BOBBY STOKES

BOBBY STOKES

The man from Portsmouth
who scored Southampton's
most famous goal

Mark Sanderson

First published by Pitch Publishing, 2016

Pitch Publishing
A2 Yeoman Gate
Yeoman Way
Worthing
Sussex
BN13 3QZ
www.pitchpublishing.co.uk

ISBN 978-1-78531-137-6

Typesetting and origination by Pitch Publishing

Printed by Bell & Bain, Glasgow, Scotland

Contents

Acknowledgements

I'D like to thank my wife Caroline, who has always encouraged me to write. We married shortly before I agreed to write this book and although she has been hugely supportive throughout the process of researching and writing it, I'm pretty sure she didn't imagine married life would result in what time we shared together being spent sat in bed with me while I watched footage of Bobby playing for the Washington Diplomats. As a full-time mum to our three-year-old daughter, and pregnant with our son during the main period of writing this book, she deserved more time and attention than I was able to give her as I submerged myself into Bobby's world. Without her support this book would not be possible. Those little tins of gin and tonic you get from the supermarket helped a great deal too.

Having carried out something in the region of 70 interviews with people who knew Bobby before, during and after his football career, I did finally speak to Bobby's family. Although I was unable to trace Bobby's ex-wife Janet – who I'm led to believe now lives abroad – I did make contact with his cousin Maria Johnson and her parents Albie and Helen Harris. Maria was kind enough to invite me to her house for a long chat between the four of us. Although I felt the material I had prior to meeting them stood on its own two feet, without their contribution this would be a far weaker book. I remain very grateful to them for being so open and generous with their time.

Thank you also to Liam Doye, who put me in touch with Bobby's old friend Jim Steele, who played with Bobby at Southampton and Washington; Jim was as gregarious and giving of his time as I could have dared to hope, sharing his contacts with me, without which I wouldn't have been able to speak with many of the leading characters in Bobby's football career. Roy Beazley was also very helpful, putting me in touch with several of Bobby's former colleagues, including Terry Paine. Sadly Roy passed away just after Christmas. David Bull at Hagiology Publishing kindly shared several transcripts of interviews relevant to Bobby's early days at The Dell.

Thanks also to Southampton supporter Mike Craft, who saved me an enormous amount of time by letting me borrow his prized collection of national newspaper cuttings featuring coverage of Southampton's 1976 FA Cup Final victory. Washington Diplomats historian and blogger Jim Reed was a great source of information on Bobby's time in the States. There were other, less orthodox, but no less memorable acts of kindness – Brian O'Neil offered to lead me in a two-car convoy on my way up the A34 to interview Mick Channon at his stables in Berkshire. While Simon Carter and Jez Gale from the Southern Daily Echo were very helpful sourcing much of the book's photography, including the cover. I'd also like to give When Saturday Comes Magazine a tip of the hat - featuring my articles over the years has encouraged me to write further. Thanks also go to Pitch Publishing for being receptive to the idea and supporting me to get the thing over the line; and last but not least, thanks goes to Bobby for the happy memories he left behind.

Foreword

THERE were times while writing this book when Bobby Stokes would appear in my dreams, stopping me in the street to ask me how I was getting on. This suggested the responsibility of writing about his life was taking its toll. Some of my early research did little to boost my confidence. The lady behind the counter of the Harbour View Café in Portsmouth, where Bobby once worked, looked confused when I told her about the book. 'Why do you want to write a book about Bobby Stokes?' she asked. Well, this is as good a place as any to explain.

Football is everywhere today. Each and every nuance of every game is picked to pieces online, on TV, radio and in the newspapers. Following that logic it would seem reasonable to expect a certain degree of prestige and posterity would be bestowed upon those who contribute to actually winning something for a club, like Bobby did when he scored Southampton's winning goal in the 1976 FA Cup Final. Many in the game have dined out on far more having achieved far less than Bobby did on that day at Wembley.

The first thing former Southampton manager Lawrie McMenemy asked me when I cold-called him at home was how I knew Bobby. I didn't. We'd never even met and

I'm not old enough to have seen him play. My motivation to write this book comes from being a Southampton supporter; one who grew up in the eastern suburbs of the city during the 1980s, a time when talk of the 1976 FA Cup Final was never too far away. The book is not an analysis of every game Bobby ever played in, nor is it a blow-by-blow account of his entire life; that would be tricky, as sadly Bobby is no longer with us to re-tell it. He is brought to life in this book through the eyes of those who knew him, it is their voices and memories that tell the story, so any error in the weaving of what they said to me can only be the fault of the weaver – namely me.

The story is as much about place as it is about Bobby's achievement. Set against the backdrop of the rivalry between the two cities of Southampton and Portsmouth – both of which Bobby is equally and intrinsically linked to – the book aims to serve as a sympathetic, but hopefully objective assessment of Bobby's life and career. On some nights when writing it, when midnight soon became one in the morning, I became very aware, perhaps even paranoid, that such objectivity was nigh on impossible for me to maintain while writing from the perspective of a Southampton supporter. But if this book can in some small way remind people of what Bobby did and what he was like as a person, then its objective will have been achieved.

Mark Sanderson

1

View From A Hill

LOOK over the edge of Portsdown Hill and Portsmouth just happens out of nowhere, rolling its way out to sea. The country roads preceding it provide none of the usual physical evidence to suggest a fast-approaching city; there are no industrial estates, retail parks, petrol stations or suburbs, just green fields rolling south until you reach that edge.

Below is Paulsgrove, a housing estate built on the hill's chalk-faced slopes, where Bobby Stokes grew up on Leominster Road in the 1950s and 60s, dreaming of becoming a professional footballer for his boyhood heroes Portsmouth. The dream came true, just not in the way he imagined it. He played briefly for Portsmouth, but Bobby is far better known for scoring the most famous goal in the history of neighbouring Southampton, who beat Manchester United in the 1976 FA Cup Final. After that his life was never the same.

Paulsgrove looks quaint from the top of Portsdown Hill. Squint down on it when the sun is shining and the terracotta-roofed houses make it look like a Spanish town somewhere in Andalucía. It's less Spanish when you get down there. A sign put up by the council in the park on Leominster Road warns that golf is banned to avoid causing nuisance to anyone else in it. Nuisance is an understatement; putting your back into the park's slope with two hands full of shopping from the Co-op at the foot of the estate can be a nuisance – having to do that while outmanoeuvring a shower of incoming golf balls is a serious pain in the arse.

The area has suffered from negative stereotypes over the years, which has left some with the impression it is an area to be best avoided. But when Bobby grew up there it was home to the working man and his family. That the council deems the anti-golf sign necessary suggests the park has already been used as a makeshift driving range. You can see why. Long and thin, much like a fairway, the park undulates at a steady 15-degree angle out towards a view of Portsmouth, where the Spinnaker Tower rises nearly 200 yards into the sky like the flag on some far-flung green.

Between the park and the tower is junction 12 of the M27, leading traffic west to Southampton and further south towards Portsmouth's ferry terminals. It's all visible to the naked eye, but it would take some tee-shot to reach these landmarks from Leominster Road – as the crow flies, the Spinnaker Tower is four miles south of Paulsgrove.

You won't find a plaque or memorial of any kind in Paulsgrove to commemorate Bobby's famous Southampton goal. These kinds of accolades are reserved for other figures. Former Prime Ministers Clement Atlee and James Callaghan have nearby roads named after them. At the top of Portsdown Hill stands Nelson's Monument – a 110-foot tribute to Britain's most famous naval leader that has stood for more than 200 years in front of panoramic views of Portsmouth and the surrounding Solent water. These views offer great perspective. Not that perspective will do you much good in Paulsgrove, especially on the subject of Southampton. Public mentions of the city are sparse round these parts.

In Paulsgrove, Southampton tends to only be referred to by name by the road signs leading you to the motorway. For many the city is called Scum, and those who play for, or support, Southampton, are Scummers. The term is based around an alleged dock strike in Portsmouth which was broken by the South Coast Union Men (SCUM) of Southampton. The acronym has stuck with many Portsmouth fans, although it's proved difficult for historians to pinpoint exactly when that strike took place, if indeed it did at all. With nobody able to reach an agreement, the entire population of Southampton continues to be labelled by some, by the actions of a mysterious group of, as yet, unidentified people, who did something nobody can be sure about at a time that cannot be confirmed.

Not that Southampton fans are innocent bystanders in the rivalry. They have their own name for Portsmouth Football Club and its fans. It's a reference to their rivals' nautical roots. So in Southampton, Portsmouth are known as the Skates – the fish whose mouth bears a sufficient enough resemblance to female genitalia. Rumour has it this part of the fish is lubricant enough to have been used by lonely seamen to relieve themselves of the growing sexual urges brought on by many months spent at sea. This handpicked image was chosen by Southampton fans to demonstrate exactly what they think of their neighbours. But the back story of the rivalry is immaterial; quite simply it wouldn't do to wear a Southampton jersey in Paulsgrove.

Walk down through the park on Leominster Road, past St Michael and All Angels Anglican Church, and the well-tended flower beds that can be seen towards the parade of shops at the foot of the estate, and you will see several Portsmouth flags flying from the windows and balconies of flats. It's not exclusively Portsmouth shirts worn in the area though. Walk into the bookies and you will see the usual mixture of Manchester United, Arsenal and Liverpool shirts. That tolerance of the colours of other club's shirts only stretches so far. Place a bet dressed in a Southampton shirt and you'd most likely be chased out of the estate through Portchester and up the A27 to the village of Titchfield and beyond.

Bobby did eventually play for Portsmouth, but the seven months he spent at Fratton Park between August 1977 and February 1978 are no more than a footnote in his career compared to the famous goal that turned him into a household name to sports fans overnight. They remember his goal and his mop of wispy hair, like a cross between a grown-up Artful Dodger and a session guitarist for The Faces. Southampton have not won a major honour since. The Johnstone's Paint Trophy they won at Wembley in 2010 does not count as the competition is only eligible to those in the lower two divisions of the Football League. Without it though, Southampton supporters under the age of 45 wouldn't know what it's like to see their team win a trophy at Wembley.

Even 45-year-olds would struggle to remember 1976. You'd have to be pushing 50 to have really experienced it. Southampton hadn't won a major honour in the 91 years of existence prior to the cup final, either. The trophy remains the only major honour the club has ever won in what is at the time of writing 131 years of football and counting. In that context, Bobby is in a league of his own. His goal remains a unique contribution to the history of the club.

Run the clock forward 19 years from 1976 and Bobby was back in his home town of Portsmouth, cooking breakfasts and serving mugs of tea in a traditional greasy spoon café on Portsmouth harbour. The years may have passed, but his goal was never far behind him. It defined the rest of his life. Seldom would a day go by when he wasn't asked about it by customers – often tourists, or journalists, who knew where to go if they needed a quote for a story relating to the FA Cup.

Bobby was proud of the goal, but he would never boast about it. Quite the contrary – he wouldn't even bring it up in conversation. Having a laugh and joke was one thing, but making out like he was the main man was beyond the pale. Still, Bobby would open up to those who showed an interest. 'I don't wear my medal around my neck, but I'll happily recall every detail of the match with anyone who has 90 minutes to spare,' said Bobby, in conversation with a reporter in early 1995. 'It was the best day of my life.' This interview was most likely to have been his last.

Those words appeared in the pages of a newspaper. In isolation they don't reveal how Bobby actually said them. If it was the best day of his life did he sing it down the telephone line? Or was he suggesting the life that followed the goal struggled to live up to the achievement? Video footage from a few years before this interview is more candid. *The Official History of The Saints* was a video commemorating the history of Southampton Football Club. Released in 1990, it features plenty of interviews with former players, the majority of which are conducted on the pitch at The Dell. The consistent overcast weather during these interviews suggests they were scheduled on the same day, so as to minimise costs.

Bobby looks smart – more so than his peers. Peter Osgood's plunging white v-neck sweater looks dated compared to Bobby's well cut grey suit, offset by a paisley tie fastened in a Windsor knot and pushed neatly into his shirt collar. The hairstyle remained the same, with his fringe dancing over his eyebrows. He knows full well what he's going to be asked about. And although he has little to add to what he said in the post-match cup final interviews in 1976, how he says it is telling. 'I'll always talk about it, but I'll never bring it up,' said Bobby, a grin spreading across his face.

His accent reveals his Hampshire roots, whereby Hampshire becomes 'Ampsher, but was it really the case that he wouldn't bring that goal up in conversation from time to time? What is life if you can't occasionally boast about scoring the winner in any cup final, let alone what some will have you believe is the most famous cup competition in the world? When pushed on the subject Bobby returns to the default interviewee mode of the footballer, firstly underplaying the achievement by suggesting it was a long time ago, then dismissing his goal as merely one of the responsibilities of his job.

'It's water under the bridge – it's a nice memory within me; especially for my family,' said Bobby. 'But on the day I suppose it was part of my job, or Ossie's [Peter Osgood's] job, or Mick Channon's job. We had to try and win and fortunately I got the goal.' Somehow, Bobby manages to take the least amount of credit possible for the goal. Deep down he was bursting with pride, then when he spoke about it in public the words that came out of his mouth couldn't rank the achievement any higher than something he was obliged to do. It's telling that in a video with a running time of just under 90 minutes Bobby's total contribution is a 20-second interview. No doubt those making the video where looking for something more substantial from him, maybe a soundbite nailing what it feels like to score in a final. That wasn't his style.

During those 20 seconds Bobby shuffles from side to side, skimming over the surface of an incident many others could and would have waxed lyrical over until the tape ran out. His eyes dart off into the distance, perhaps waiting for his old friend Peter Osgood to join him for a round of golf, followed by a drink or two.

Bobby had separated from his wife shortly before Christmas 1994. His health then began to deteriorate. By May 1995, his family were concerned about his ability to look after himself. Maria Johnson was Bobby's cousin and, as owner of the Harbour View Café, his co-worker. But their relationship was closer that that. Having grown up on the same Paulsgrove estate in a tight-knit family she was more of a sister to Bobby. 'I knew he wasn't right, he went downhill after his marriage broke down,' said Maria, who convinced him to stay at his parents' house, back in Leominster Road, in order to convalesce. The family rallied around. Bobby's mother Marjorie kept a bedside vigil, with his aunt Helen on hand to offer further support. Maria remembers having spaghetti bolognese and talking to Bobby about Elvis Presley one evening. The next morning Helen went to the bathroom to empty the bowl of water she had used to wash Bobby in bed with when she heard him breathing heavily. Panic set in. She ran into the bedroom, attempting to resuscitate Bobby while screaming out to his dad for help as she telephoned for an ambulance. Bobby's mother couldn't face going up the stairs. The paramedics broke the news to Helen in the bathroom. They said it was too late, there was nothing they could do. Bobby was dead. Four months earlier he had turned 44. Bobby spent his final days being cared for by those he loved most, but Maria sensed something, 'I think he knew he was going to go.'

At first, it was suspected Bobby had died of a heart attack. The post-mortem established the cause of death as bronchopneumonia. Several different groups of people are at risk of that infection, including those who smoke and drink alcohol. There were times towards the end of his life when Bobby did both. Chinese whispers often implied

BOBBY STOKES

Bobby's death was a direct result of cigarettes and alcohol, or to be more precise, that unconsciously or not he had declared some kind of war of attrition on himself which led to his death; but like so many aspects of Bobby's life, the reality was lost amid rumours and half-truths.

2

Knock-out Blow

BOBBY is held in high regard by his old teammates; nobody had a bad word to say about him. Undeterred, I kept looking. Not to paint him in a bad light, just to make sure I had an objective point of view. How many people can honestly say nobody took a dislike to them in their entire life? Even Mother Teresa got on some people's wick, so it came as something of a relief to speak to former Southampton goalkeeper Eric Martin. The Scot left The Dell to join the Washington Diplomats more than 40 years ago. He still lives in the US, watching Southampton regularly on cable TV. He said Bobby could be a bit of an asshole, as well as having a bit of an attitude. At last some dirt? No, not exactly; actually, not at all. Eric's descriptions need to be put into very clear context. Isolating them like this without any further explanation would be libel. It would also be unrepresentative of Eric's feelings. He was as fond of 'Stokesy' as everyone else.

Eric was referring very specifically to the notorious England versus Scotland five-a-side games that used to be played on Friday mornings in the tiny gym at The Dell during the 1960s and 70s. He remembers them well. 'It could get crazy,' he said. 'There was a lot of pride at stake.' Both teams showed a complete disregard for their chances of playing in the next day's game by winding each other up and kicking lumps out of one another. Behaving like an asshole was the bare minimum requirement for anyone hoping to walk out of those games in one piece. Ask Hugh Fisher. Around 5ft 7in and a very nice man, he too stepped some way over the line during those games.

Southampton's gym was similar to The Dell – tight and compact. 'It was like a bear pit,' said Hugh. The goings-on demonstrated that the club was nothing if not inclusive in those days. As a Welshman, Ron Davies discovered it didn't matter if you weren't English or Scottish – it didn't even matter if you were six-foot plus and had the word 'big' stuck in front of your name every time you were mentioned; you could still get punched in the face. Such was the feeling that notions of common sense and self-preservation went out of the window. What other possible explanation is there for Hugh drawing blood from Ron. So how did the red mist descend over Hugh? They were playing a five-a-side in the gym as usual. Hugh was trapped against a wall with the ball at his feet, but Ron Davies showed no sympathy, kicking Hugh in the back of the legs. Something snapped inside of Hugh and he turned around and let Davies have it. Denis Hollywood remembers Bobby doing exactly the same thing, bringing Davies, a much bigger man than Bobby, to his knees with a right hook. Similarly small in stature to Hugh, there was no doubting Bobby's determination on the field.

As far as Mick Channon was concerned Bobby was a good guy off the pitch, but fierce on it. 'He was a right little competitor,' insisted Mick. 'He could put his foot in and hold his own with the best of them.' On both occasions Ron Davies put his hand to his mouth and noticed he was bleeding. Fortunately for both Bobby and Hugh there were four or five other team-mates holding Ron back before he was able to dish out his own retribution, which is no doubt what he had planned judging by his cries of 'I'll kill him'. Incidents like these were regular occurrences and all forgotten about afterwards. Well, until the next Friday morning five-a-side at least.

Bobby really was held in high regard by everyone he knew. Talking on the subject his ex-playing colleagues would say pretty much the same thing, that he was a 'tremendous little fella', and that you would do well to find anyone who didn't think the same thing. News of his death came as a great shock to many of those former team-mates. Tommy O'Hara became close friends with Bobby during their time together playing for the Washington Diplomats. An unsolicited telephone call to Tommy disturbed his journey to a dental appointment, as well as agitating old wounds. Simply talking about Bobby caused his voice on one occasion to tail off, as though still coming to terms with the loss.

Mick Channon is Southampton's all-time leading goalscorer. He talks freely about Bobby until you remind him of the 20 years plus that have passed since his death. He shakes his head and sighs. Remind him too of how old Bobby was when he died and he swears under his breath like only Mick Channon can swear – in that thick Wiltshire burr. 'Bobby was everybody's mate – he was a smashing lad,' said Mick. 'If you had a problem with him as a person then there was something wrong with you.'

Nick Holmes, another of Bobby's Southampton team-mates from the 1976 FA Cup Final, was disturbed by the news. He had no idea there was anything wrong with Bobby. Nobody has played more games for Southampton than Terry Paine, who found out about Bobby's death when reading the story in a newspaper. Terry found it difficult to accept the words he was reading; that someone he remembered so full of life could die at such a young age didn't seem real. But Terry was living in South Africa at the time, having moved there a decade beforehand, so his memories of Bobby remained firmly rooted in the past when Bobby was still a fit and healthy young man.

To others, there were warning signs of Bobby's failing health. While the news hit former team-mate Brian O'Neil hard, he was not truly shocked by it. He was with Bobby not long before he died. They sat in the back of a hired limousine en route to the opening night of Celebration Plaza, a bar in Southampton owned by Matt Le Tissier during the 1990s, when Brian told Bobby the two of them should write a book, not to settle any scores, but about all the laughs they'd had over the years. Bobby looked gaunt and ashen. There was no colour in his face. Back in his Southampton playing days, Brian and Bobby used to go down to the dog track in Portsmouth on a Friday before a Southampton home game, usually calling in on Bobby's parents in Paulsgrove afterwards. Brian wanted to say hello to them at the funeral, but he didn't get the chance – it was packed. By the time he arrived at Portchester Crematorium he did well to find a place to stand at the back of the chapel.

Go there today and your nostrils are overcome by a musty smell of undisturbed papers and documents. A small wooden sign inside the chapel asks for silence against the backdrop of heavy red velvet drapes. It comes as a relief to leave the building for the well-maintained lawns outside. Any irony over the organ player chugging their way through a rendition of 'When the Saints go Marching In' in what is a Portsmouth stronghold was lost during Bobby's funeral. Rivalry had no place here. 'Abide With Me', the traditional hymn of the FA Cup Final, was also played so that an occasion which defined Bobby during his life would do so again in death.

Jim Steele played alongside Bobby in the cup final, and in the US. He read the eulogy at the funeral. It focused on how he thought Bobby would want everybody to remember the good times they shared with him, rather than dwell on anything morbid. And there were plenty of good times. It looked like there were more to come. Prior to his death, word had got around that perhaps all was not well financially with Bobby. Southampton had offered him a benefit year in 1994. It was due to climax with a testimonial match at The Dell, which was to feature a who's who of previous Southampton star players. Bobby had opened up to reporters about how the benefit year came about. 'After being at The Dell for more than ten years I was disappointed at the time not to get a testimonial,' he said. 'Then one day I thought I'd just brass-neck it and ask. In the end all it cost me was a 20-pence phonecall.'

The thought of Bobby having to ask for his own party is a bit of a sad one. You wonder how many times he might have picked up the telephone to call the club, maybe having scribbled down his lines, practising how he would go about pitching the idea, before thinking better of it and returning to the frying pan and the tea urn of the Harbour View Café where he worked. In Southampton's defence, they hadn't gone out of their way to ostracise Bobby. Time had just moved on in what is, despite many fans' beliefs, a very unsentimental business. Bobby did spend 11 years with Southampton – one more than necessary to justify a testimonial match, usually needed by players who wouldn't have earned anywhere near enough money during their playing careers to spend their days improving their golf handicap, let alone retire. In the 1970s players were doing a job people would love to do. The pay was far from terrible, but it wasn't enough to not work after retiring from the game, as Bobby explained: 'I was never on more than £100 a week basic at The Dell, but we had good incentives and if everything went well and I scored some goals on a good week I could earn £300.'

However, those 11 years he spent at Southampton included two as an apprentice. He didn't sign professionally until 1968, so to the letter of the law Southampton hadn't actually wronged him. But given his goal had given them their finest hour, perhaps they could have done more. But that's hindsight. In the end the club had sanctioned a testimonial, it was just unfortunate Bobby never lived to see it. A few letters in the local press insisted the game should go ahead to remember him by, despite his death. But once he had gone any idea to play that game in his memory fell flat. Those relying on the obituaries and newspaper reports to form an accurate picture of Bobby's life would have been left wanting. A report in *Portsmouth News* listed one of his previous jobs as a cab driver. This would have demonstrated a very cavalier approach to the law, if of course it was true. As part of a promotion Bobby won a Ford Granada for scoring the FA Cup Final winner at Wembley, but he never had a driving licence. It's rumoured that when the public relations people from Ford went into the dressing room to give Bobby the good news, he looked perplexed. Car? What did Bobby want a car for? He didn't drive.

The stories at the time of his death revealed other far less trivial and more pressing uncertainties. They described him as a happy man, never miserable, while others claimed the real cause of his death was a broken heart. The *Southern Daily Echo* and *Portsmouth News* both featured glowing tributes to Bobby. Not simply as a footballer, but as a person. The name Bobby Stokes will always be associated with the FA Cup Final, but that still doesn't tell us anything about the man. There seems to be a widely held perception that Bobby's footballing career petered out after leaving Southampton. It's true that it didn't reach quite the same heights, but in many ways neither did the careers of any of the other members of the Southampton starting XI. Only one other player from that side went on to play in another winning cup final team – that was Mick Channon for Norwich City, who won the League Cup in 1985. The lack of further trophies isn't limited to that group of players. On occasions in the last 40 years, Southampton have danced around success without ever actually achieving it. But still Bobby's move to the Washington Diplomats of the North American Soccer League (NASL) was deemed to be something close to semi-retirement. This is both unfair and untrue. Far from being a retirement home for ageing stars, the North American Soccer League (NASL), which Bobby left Southampton to join in 1977, was a progressive and forward thinking place, where games were played in state of the art stadiums in the US in front of much more relaxed family crowds, with and against some of the greatest players to have ever played, including Pelé, Franz Beckenbauer, Carlos Alberto, Johan Cruyff and Johan Neeskens.

It was a world away from the dilapidated stadiums of England's top two divisions, which were often blighted by hooliganism. That is not to say Bobby's career was on a complete upward trajectory when he left England. His summer seasons spent in Washington were interspersed with winter seasons back in England for clubs of an ever decreasing quality. Having shared a dressing room with Johan Cruyff at Washington during the summer he would return to England in the winter to play outside the Football League with Cheltenham Town and Chichester City. What remained consistent was what others thought of him. He was well liked, loved even. But in the end that seemed to be of little use to him.

Jim McCalliog made the precision pass that created Bobby's goal at Wembley. He was one of very few of

Bobby's former playing colleagues who didn't want to be interviewed for this book. He wasn't rude, far from it, but he was firm and to the point: he didn't want to be involved. Jim complained of people trying to make money from his name – through autographs, football shirts and general football memorabilia. 'My football career was 40 years ago, I just want to get on with my life now,' said Jim, before saying he thought Bobby was a special guy. He finished by telling me I could write him a letter with more details about the book if I really wanted. I never did. Not out of spite or any bad feeling; it just didn't seem necessary. Without saying very much Jim had revealed a great deal.

Winning the FA Cup in 1976 was as fantastic for Jim McCalliog as it was for Bobby. Jim had scored the opening goal of the 1966 FA Cup Final while still a teenager playing for Sheffield Wednesday, but their two-goal lead was clawed back by Everton, who ended up winning 3-2. Jim would turn 30 in the latter part of 1976. Chances to win this or any other trophy were running out for him. Winning the FA Cup in 1976 was redemption, but being forever tethered to that moment brought its own baggage. There were those who wanted to piggy-back the success. That could be a drag. There was always someone who wanted a piece of you, it could be exhausting. Bobby's smile would remain, although at times he too felt the weight of responsibility that his goal carried with it.

Bobby's parents, along with his brother David, his uncle Albie, aunt Helen and cousin Maria, scattered his ashes on the centre circle at The Dell, Southampton's idiosyncratic home for 103 years. Paulsgrove was always home, but in many ways so was The Dell. Meeting the requirements of the Taylor Report meant crowbarring plastic seating into the ground's old concrete stands in the mid-1990s, leaving it open to ridicule that a Premier League club could play in such a place, which by then was only able to accommodate 15,000 fans. The ground was demolished for housing in 2001 as the club moved to St Mary's, a new all-seater stadium on the other side of town. The housing built in place of The Dell replicates the ground it replaced, with town houses and flats making a perimeter around a residential car park. Within the middle of that car park is a small patch of grass, most likely to have been the centre circle at the old stadium. This small patch is hemmed in by a concrete wall, which is indented with the soles of football boots – a football-themed motif by Barratt Homes.

The four sides of housing surrounding the car park are named after Ted Bates, Mick Channon, Matt Le Tissier and the Wallace brothers (Ray, Rod and Danny), with a further block of flats just outside that rectangle named after Bobby, which is the only reminder of his memory in Southampton, while the small patch of grass at the grounds of what was The Dell is his final resting place. Of course, neither Barratt Homes, nor Southampton, were under any obligation to turn what was The Dell into any shrine to the footballing past, but it's doubtful many, if any, Southampton fans were aware this was where Bobby's ashes were scattered. Go there today and on the rare occasion anyone does occupy that grass in the middle of the car park they study those studded indents on the shallow concrete wall as if trying to decipher some ancient form of hieroglyphics. There is no meaning or explanation to them; it's merely a token gesture. It needn't have been that way.

3

Skates And Scummers

TO understand the rivalry between Southampton and Portsmouth is to understand Bobby's life as a Portsmouth resident before and after his FA Cup Final-winning goal for Southampton at Wembley. He would often end an afternoon playing for Southampton with a pint or two in Portsmouth. Having showered and changed he caught the train home to Southsea, stopping off in Portsmouth's Guildhall Walk. The idea the man responsible for scoring Southampton's most famous goal was sinking a few cold ones in the heartlands of their bitter rivals is difficult for those who tie their colours to one of two local masts to understand. It went further than that though. Bobby would mix with the opposition. Like Bobby, Keith Viney was originally from Paulsgrove, as well as being a young Portsmouth full-back, when he would share a few drinks with Bobby on those Saturday afternoons between 1975 and 1977. Such a thing actually wasn't that unusual if at a neutral venue, but not here in Portsmouth city centre and not in broad daylight.

No other Southampton players would be indulged that liberty. Take Francis Benali as an example. He gained cult-like status without ever being Southampton's hottest property. Although in recent years his status at the club has been elevated to legend, this may have more to do with his recent masochistic running regime in aid of Cancer Research, which ended at a packed St Mary's Stadium rather than his performances in a red and white Southampton shirt. Some of his contributions to matches during the 1990s would invoke a few cross word from the terraces, but during the course of that decade he became almost as synonymous with the club as Matt Le Tissier.

Of course, Benali wasn't fit to lace Le Tissier's boots, and that was the whole point. In many ways he, more than anyone else, came to epitomise Southampton's bitter struggle in maintaining their place in the English top flight. For every Le Tissier wonder goal there would be a whole-hearted Benali challenge, sometimes ending up with the ball in his own net, or being sent off, but his actions were always carried out with one hundred per cent commitment in the cause of the city he was born in. This is why fans could identify with him. This also explains why he is equally despised by some in Portsmouth. For those in blue, Benali is not a legend; he was a left-back with limited abilities who somehow kept his head above water during a 16-year career spent in England's First Division and then Premier League.

The irony is that Benali's determination is exactly the kind of achievement that would be respected in Portsmouth if only it were achieved in a blue, rather than a red and white shirt. The truth doesn't always fit the narrative being sung from the terraces. Who you support is largely dependent on where you are born and who your parents follow. Of course there are season ticket holders at each club whose children support their rival, but such things can only happen in the fringes, in the suburbs between the two cities, where you can see men in opposing club's merchandise pass one another in the supermarket aisles without so much as a word being exchanged. The idea of such a thing actually happening in either city wouldn't be given the oxygen to develop.

In short, if Benali was seen in Cascades Shopping Centre in Portsmouth there would be a riot. Matt Le Tissier wouldn't even get that far. He would be taking his life into his hands if headed east past junction 11 of the M27. Nobody ever gave Bobby a hard time for that Saturday beer in Portsmouth. Nor did Keith ever get criticised for fraternising so publicly with the local rivals, as he explains, 'Back then I don't think players were as easily recognisable as they are today. Once or twice people would notice us, but they soon realised Bobby was a Pompey lad at heart and he never said anything bad about the place, so he was forgiven for playing for Southampton.'

Forgiveness in Portsmouth requires its own very specific context. The city is a more hostile environment than Southampton. This is not to suggest Southampton is one big estate of five-bed mock Tudor mansions, it's more to do with geography. Portsmouth is effectively an island; it's more difficult to escape. Unless leaving by sea you only really have two outlets – via the M275 in the west or the A27 to the east. Whereas Southampton blends out gently into the Hampshire suburbs, in which up until recently Portsmouth trained on a daily basis. This meant seeing Portsmouth players in Southampton wasn't a totally alien experience, particularly where public transport was concerned. Their training base was Wellington Sports Ground just a few miles outside Southampton city centre, where Southampton had originally planned to build their new stadium. It meant you could on occasions see John Utaka, a member of Portsmouth's 2008 FA Cup-winning team, alight the platform at nearby Southampton Airport Parkway station.

The ill feeling between the two cities isn't confined to matchdays. Evidence of it can crop up in the most unusual of places. Go to the second floor of Portsmouth Library, past the giant bust of Charles Dickens, towards a wall of filing cabinets carefully packed with countless reels of negatives, containing archived copies of the *Portsmouth News* since it began publication. By a strange quirk of coincidence the reel of film for May 1976, which one would assume would have details of Southampton's 1976 FA Cup Final victory, is missing. I took this up with the librarian but the idea that somebody – presumably a Portsmouth supporter – had removed it from the premises on account of being unable to stomach a record of Southampton's finest hour being stored in one of Portsmouth's foremost centres of learning was politely dismissed as fantasy. They were still unable to find that reel though. With such a huge and public record of data it was sadly inevitable that one or two items would go missing. That this particular record was missing seemed more than coincidence.

The spread of hooliganism across the UK in the 1970s probably helped to liven things up between the two cities. By which time, it was Southampton and not Portsmouth who were playing in England's top division. There seemed to be a consensus among some Portsmouth supporters that Southampton's attendances, both home and away, weren't worthy of First Division football. That they hadn't gone through enough of a struggle to merit the privilege of top flight football – it was almost wasted on them. Portsmouth had suffered. By 1978 they had been relegated to the Fourth Division; so 28 years after being champions of England they weren't just playing Grimsby,

Halifax and Torquay – they were losing to them too. Go to Fratton Park or St Mary's and chances are you will hear a significant number of supporters chanting about how they hate their rival club. Not everyone subscribes to the view that the other team is to be despised at all costs. By the same token, not everyone who does hold that view is in the habit of arranging a punch-up at a quiet industrial estate.

The distance between the two cities means the sight of someone dressed in a rival's replica jersey is something of a novelty. With no shortage of online fan forums and message boards, people can jabber on defiantly about how they hate the other. There's safety in numbers, especially under the anonymity of a pseudonym. That said, the rivalry is there and in many areas it is fierce. The Cascades was as off limits for Nick Holmes as it was for Francis Benali. He played nearly 500 games for Southampton, growing up supporting the club before making his debut alongside Bobby against Arsenal at Highbury in 1974. He was at The Dell when Bobby played his first game in 1969. Nick and his dad had season tickets. He remembers envying Bobby, who as a teenager, wasn't much older than Nick, for doing what he was doing. It wouldn't be long until they were team-mates. Nick questions whether the derby games are played in the same kind of environment as he remembers experiencing in the 1970s and 80s. 'I didn't hate Portsmouth but I knew full well how important it was to win those games. We didn't play each other a lot when I was there, but those games were the most nerve-wracking of any. I've been to the derby games in the 2000s and I don't think there is the same intensity in the games I played.'

While it is hyped up now, the rivalry has been there for a while. Terry Paine experienced the intensity first-hand as much as anyone, but he doesn't understand the hatred between the two sets of fans. 'Sure, you want to beat them,' insists Terry. 'But I'd like to see all south coast clubs in the Premier League; imagine the derby games and the atmosphere.' It has been documented that the night before derby games in Division Two during the 1960s, Terry would receive an anonymous telephone call from a Portsmouth supporter. Terry laughs at the memory. 'The phone would ring and a monotonous voice would say, "Hello, is that Terry Paine? Roy Lunniss is going to get you tomorrow." Then they'd hang up.'

Roy Lunniss was a tall Portsmouth full-back, who wasn't afraid of a good old-fashioned battle with whoever he was marking in a game. 'All part and parcel of the game of course,' said Terry. Although frankly, the idea that a team's star player would get an anonymous call on his landline seems to cross the line between rivalry and harassment. But Terry took it in good spirit. And that's what rivalry means to him – it's about competitive spirit, nothing more. The rivalry can do strange things to people. It's all too easy to get caught up in the vortex when 30,000 people share a confined space.

Bobby played in the derby for Southampton six times during the 1970s, only losing once, at Fratton Park in May 1975. This was also the only time he scored in the fixture, a header, with only three minutes left in the game. It wasn't enough to stop Southampton losing 2-1. Only 5,000 were there to see it though because rather than a competitive fixture, it was a testimonial match, in this case for Portsmouth's Ray Hiron.

Testimonials between the two sides were relatively common during that time but there has not been one since Alan Knight's at Fratton Park in 1994. The horseplay on the field, which saw Knight score a penalty, and Portsmouth momentarily have 12 players on the field against an opposition including Alan Ball in the Southampton midfield, wasn't recognised by some on the terraces, who charged towards the Southampton fans after the final whistle. Relations between the two sets of fans probably weren't helped by the fact that Southampton had won the game 5-1.

In the last 50 years Southampton have enjoyed relative success, in that they have spent the majority of that time in England's top division. A host of household names, from Alan Ball, Kevin Keegan, Peter Shilton, Alan Shearer and Gareth Bale, have all worn the red-and-white-striped shirt. But, unlike Portsmouth, who have two league titles and two FA Cups to their name, Southampton have won just the one major honour in 131 years. Bobby's goal was responsible for that trophy, so it's not unreasonable to expect a bit more of a song and dance to have been made about him in the city.

There used to be a suite at Southampton's St Mary's Stadium named after Bobby. It was capable of holding 50 people and advertised in the club's hospitality brochures as an ideal venue for sales meetings and seminars. In reality it wasn't much to look at. The most eye-catching feature of the room was the carpet, a garish combination of green and red that you can imagine salesmen looking into trance-like during one of those seminars. Bobby's picture hung on the wall – a pseudo pop art canvas, the kind of thing you could probably pick up on eBay for £20. Not terrible, but perhaps not fitting enough to commemorate such a significant moment. Surely the club would be better advised to obtain some original photography to put on show, having invested in a decent frame. The suite was at least a focal point in the stadium dedicated to Bobby. Now there is nothing.

The suite was rebranded under the regime of former executive chairman Nicola Cortese. This followed a trend whereby Cortese fell out with several of the club's former stars. At the time the club was on the up after a few dreadful years which nearly saw it liquidated in 2009. The late Swiss businessman Marcus Liebherr came in and bought the club for what he described as *ein Schnäppchen* (a bargain). Liebherr appointed Nicola Cortese as executive chairman. When Liebherr passed away in 2010, Cortese took on the role of fulfilling the Liebherr family's wishes. The objective was to return to the Premier League – a noble aim, which seemed pretty far-fetched at a time when the club were sharing a division with Yeovil Town and Wycombe Wanderers.

Cortese proved himself to be committed and ruthless. He did not seem at all fazed by making unpopular decisions like sacking Alan Pardew, and later his replacement Nigel Adkins. The club's fans were furious but the anger soon subsided once both new managers began to steer the club to good results; as Adkins replaced Pardew, and Mauricio Pochettino replaced Adkins. Whether or not the decisions were morally correct they were vindicated by the results on the field. Fans will hold no grudge with the past as long as the present offers a better alternative. Under Cortese, South-ampton fans would stomach almost anything – even red shorts as part of the home kit. The fans could be forgiven. Having stared oblivion in the face, they were still just glad to have a club to support, so tampering with traditional elements of the kit passed muster without too much fuss.

Having been through the mill, fans seemed to enjoy having a no-nonsense character in charge. He was built of different stuff than some of the pencil-necks of the past. If he was lacking in anything it appeared to be a sense of humour. Or at least this was the perception. It's entirely possible that in private he spends his spare time cracking up over repeats of *Only Fools and Horses*. His public image makes that a bit of a stretch of the imagination. It's more plausible his preferred hobby was to throw darts at pictures of Matt Le Tissier – who was no longer welcome at the club for criticising Cortese's sacking of Nigel Adkins in 2013 – and former manager Lawrie McMenemy, whose framed photograph that had once adorned the walls of St Mary's had been rumoured to have been taken down at Cortese's specific request.

But Cortese's rift with the club's past seemed to run deeper than a bun fight. The implication from the administration was that they didn't want anyone from yesteryear enjoying a free lunch at the club's expense. Every pound spent needed to be justified. Perhaps the responsibility of doing the very best job weighed heavy on Cortese's shoulders. With that in mind, maybe he could be forgiven for his lack of sense of humour, but in hindsight maybe he would have been better off if he'd developed a better bedside manner. First and foremost results on the field provide stability. But a football club is underpinned by its identity, which in turn is born out of its heritage. These are marketable assets. So far from being sentimental, building bridges to the successes of the past can be good for business.

A great deal of clubs throughout the country employ ex-players as comperes in hospitality suites. It's a mutually beneficial relationship. Ex-players get to earn a few quid for retelling stories of yesteryear and fans get to revel in those stories and share a drink with the players they still look up to. It's surely one of the very few reasons to justify the extortionate prices clubs charge for tickets in hospitality for what is essentially watching a game of football with a hot dinner. Many fans would like that experience enriched by sharing it with the likes of say Jim Steele and Mark Dennis – two former Southampton players with colourful pasts, which is exactly what is needed when telling the tales of their careers.

Cortese isn't involved any longer but the club has yet to do anything to rectify the lack of commemoration to

Bobby. Not that it is obliged to do so. But for what has always been known as a family club, it seems odd that there is no reference to the past, if only to serve as a spur for future players on what has been achieved before and what is expected in the future. At present, the names of each stand at St Mary's are functional, representing the names of the areas in the city they face out to. The club have had players who have made lasting contributions to its history.

The leverage of the past could be used to rename those stands. Of course, naming a stand after the man who'd made the highest number of appearances for the club, Terry Paine, might throw up a certain anomaly. You don't really want supporters saying they've been sat in Paine for the entire season. But would his achievement of more than 800 games for the club be fitting of a stand being named after him, whereby the Itchen Stand were to be renamed the Terry Paine right wing? The same could be said for Mick Channon, Matt Le Tissier and of course Bobby Stokes.

Bobby played at a time when trying to win something amounted to more than the lure of any money gained from finishing towards the top of the league table. If you took a straw poll of Southampton fans old enough to remember the 1975/76 season it's unlikely many will remember where the team finished in the final Second Division table that year. For the record, it was sixth, sandwiched between Notts County, who were a place above on goal difference, and Luton Town, who finished below with a point less.

The FA Cup Final was not always the great game that history sometimes leads you to believe. But perceptions have to be put into context – it was one of very few games shown live on television, so there was a huge appetite for it. The competition was then still able to create a scenario whereby Bobby Stokes – a good player, but not a superstar

– could score the winning goal in a game that anyone with a passing interest in the game would watch.

It's not difficult to see why many get dewy-eyed in nostalgia for the competition's past when pragmatism now too often wins out over glory. Mauricio Pochettino was popular during his short spell as manager, but his team selection in the FA Cup against Sunderland in 2014 felt like a waving of the white flag. His job was not to protect the heritage of the past but to some his approach to that game was an indictment of the current state of the competition. It is something that has to be fitted in among a busy fixture list, so that the chances of another Bobby Stokes scoring the cup final winner remain as likely as a player ignoring a stomach upset, as Bobby did, to score an important equalising goal away to West Bromwich Albion in the fifth round of that season's run to glory.

With 40 years having passed, Southampton fans old enough to remember the 1976 FA Cup Final no doubt carry Bobby's memory in their hearts and minds, but there is no physical reminder in the city. Memories grow dimmer. Who was Bobby Stokes? As time passes an ever fewer group of people will be able to answer that question.

4

Paulsgrove

BLOOD ran down Kevin Wallace's face. He'd been stood at the front of a queue of other nine-year-old boys, all waiting their turn to bat in a game of cricket being played during breaktime at Hillside Junior School in Paulsgrove. In their eagerness, the boys in the queue had edged ever closer behind the current batsman, who took an almighty swing. This was quickly followed by a familiar cracking sound that seemed destined to result in the ball being sent far over the heads of what looked like 100 fielders dotted around the playground. Instead the ball rolled harmlessly behind the stumps. For the first and only time during that game nobody paid any attention to the ball. They were far more interested in the small hole in Kevin's head and how much more blood could possibly pour out of it.

More than 50 years later the scar remains – a small crescent shape above Kevin's left eye; as does the memory of the words of a ginger-haired kid – whose name he has long since forgotten – who, as Kevin sank to his knees to stem the flow of blood, turned towards the batsman and said, 'Ere, Bobby – you've cut his fucking 'ead open.'

Kevin was carted off by a dinner lady. Meanwhile, the cricket recommenced on the playground, although to be on the safe side the batting queue gave the batsman a bit more breathing space. Word got round that Kevin had gone to hospital for stitches. That evening there was a knock on his door. From the lounge he could hear a lady ask his mum if he was in. He walked into the hallway and saw a face he recognised. It was Bobby Stokes. Bobby's mum Marjorie had frogmarched him to Kevin's house to apologise for cutting his head open with a cricket bat. Bobby stood silent in the doorway, looking down towards his shoes. 'Go on, then,' said Bobby's mum, poking him in the arm. Bobby apologised. Kevin's house in Camcross Close was only a 15-minute walk from Bobby's on Leominster Road, but the walk there would have felt a lot longer that night, no doubt having to rehearse his lines of apology in front of his mum. Kevin calls the accident his claim to fame and will happily share the day the man who scored the winning goal in an FA Cup Final scarred him for life with anyone who will listen.

As far as Kevin was concerned, when it came to sport Bobby stood out from all the others at school. 'Sports day was Bobby Stokes day,' he said. That may have been, but it was evident this didn't give him licence to do as he pleased without a telling-off. Of course, it had been an accident – Bobby hadn't meant to hurt Kevin. But accident or not it didn't mean he could forego taking responsibility for what he'd done. It was perhaps in this grounded working-class environment that the seeds were sown to prevent Bobby from ever becoming big-headed. Sport played a big part in the lives of the kids in Paulsgrove. Today there is a sign on the long, narrow patch of grass in Camcross Close that says 'no ball games'. This wouldn't have done much to stop them back then. The landscape was their sports field, lamp-posts were makeshift wickets and they would play in the streets until someone, perhaps fed up of stray balls hitting their windows panes, would tell them to clear off.

Portsmouth was bombed during the Second World War. Many families were rehoused in Paulsgrove, a housing estate built after the war, which wasn't entirely finished until the early 1950s. Many of the houses were prefabricated and could be put up in less than a week. The area had plenty of pubs.

Most of the pubs in the area from back then – like The Sociable Plover – no longer exist. The sign at The Old House at Home remains, but it is now housing. A few weeds sprout from the car park; being a listed English building the original pub still stands. Other pubs haven't been as fortunate. The Beacon and The Beehive were both demolished in the last 20 years, the former having been closed by the police after rumoured escalating violence by its clientele. The pub was later set on fire. The Clacton Arms was also set on fire. All three pubs have been replaced by housing. Other than the Grove Social Club at the foot of the hill there is only one pub in Paulsgrove left – The Cross Keys. But Kevin Wallace remembers his dad, like many others, would spend pretty much Friday night until Sunday in the pubs and betting shops. Then Monday came along and it was time for work once more, so another drink might not pass their lips until the following Friday. There was a certain kind of discipline in that routine. Although Kevin's mum might have something to say about that, as would many of the wives of the men on the estate.

Bobby's dad was not a drinking man. The only time alcohol passed David Stokes's lips was on Christmas Day when he toasted everyone a merry Christmas with a tiny drop of Bailey's. The Stokes household on Leominster Road backed on to the house in which Albie and Helen

Harris, Bobby's uncle and aunt, lived. Helen and Bobby's mother Marjorie were two of 16 brothers and sisters, but the bond between the two was a long-lasting and rich relationship that saw Bobby and his elder brother David spend as much time with Albie and Helen as they did their own parents. Albie and Helen's daughter, Bobby's cousin Maria, did likewise with Bobby's parents.

David Stokes senior exemplified the working man of the time. Helen Harris describes her brother-in-law as a gentleman, 'You'd never ever hear him swear.' Bobby and his brother played tennis on the local courts after school and David would pick them up. Bobby didn't realise his dad was nearby. 'He said something like sod or bugger and turned round and saw his dad,' added Helen. Bobby was frogmarched home – swearing in any form wasn't tolerated. 'So you can imagine how I got on,' joked Albie.

'Dad swears like a trooper, so did our Marjorie,' said Maria. 'But I never heard uncle Dave swear.' If Bobby's dad heard his wife Marjie curse he would tut, saying something along the lines of, Marjorie, please, we can't have that. 'He never had a holiday, all he thought about was his home and his family,' said Helen, who was very close to Bobby. 'He's still with us every day, he was like a son to us.' But to his family Bobby wasn't Bobby at all, he was Rob, or Robbie. Maria cannot remember who the first person was to call him Bob or Bobby, 'We always called him Rob.' Years later when the two worked together at the Harbour View Café locals would be confused by Maria calling the man they knew as Bobby by another name. 'They would turn around and wonder who I was talking to,' said Maria. '"Don't you mean Bobby," they said.' She didn't.

Like Kevin Wallace, Steve Hatton went to primary school with Bobby. He was part of a family of five children who were rehoused in Paulsgrove during the early 1950s, 'We were all working families in the area, but we weren't well off – money was scarce. It wasn't unusual for kids to have cornflake packets put in their shoes to cover the holes in their soles,' said Steve. He thinks this would probably have been common in many working-class areas in post-war Britain. It was a time of make do and mend and jumble sales.

Holidays away were unheard of, so when it became known Steve's neighbours were going on holiday in Wales it came as something of a shock. What the community lacked in material wealth it had in other riches. As someone who went on to become a teacher himself, Steve recognised that the children at Hillside during his school days were fortunate. 'We had teachers who were worldly wise – they didn't need a syllabus to keep us occupied,' said Steve, who thinks their ex-service background might have helped in this regard.

Like Kevin Wallace, Steve wasn't as sporty as Bobby. 'He was good at all sports – you name it he could do it,' said Steve. 'Even cricket ball throwing – *the bastard*,' laughed Steve, getting across the hopelessness of trying to compete against him in sport. Like many boys, Steve often played football with Bobby on the sloped park on Leominster Road. 'So many of us played that sometimes it felt like it was 40-a-side; it was the same at breaktime at school – we'd make do playing with a rolled-up pair of gloves,' added Steve.

These children were born into a world where Portsmouth were defending league champions. When Bobby was born in January 1951 Portsmouth were actually double league champions, retaining the title they had won five points ahead of Manchester United in 1949, by beating Wolverhampton Wanderers on goal difference in 1950. It's worth labouring the point: Portsmouth won back-to-back titles, a feat only ten other clubs have ever done. They have sunk to some sorry depths in their time, but have also tasted the highest of highs.

Those glory days could have been better still – the double of Football League championship and FA Cup looked a strong possibility for Portsmouth in 1949. Seeing as they'd put five goals past Everton at Goodison Park it stood to reason that they could take care of Second Division Leicester City in the FA Cup semi-final at Highbury. Don Revie had other ideas. Long before he became manager of Leeds United and England, he was an attacking player and his performance inspired Leicester to beat Portsmouth 3-1. Portsmouth would win the FA Cup again, but they would have to wait until 2008 to do so. The achievement seems to have fallen through the cracks of time for anybody who doesn't follow Portsmouth. It's as though winning back-to-back titles before the advent of colour television makes it somehow obsolete, which is ridiculous, of course – it is a feat any club would be proud of.

Many other clubs have achieved less in more recent years, but they are able to dust off the televised, and often colour, footage like an old comfort blanket. Today, seeing is believing; if it cannot be looked up on YouTube it may as well not exist. For Bobby, the days of back-to-back titles at Fratton Park might as well have been during the time of another Portsmouth-born figure, Charles Dickens. He was too young to remember. His experience of glory would have been a vicarious one – listening to the words of his friends' fathers talking of the days when 'Jolly' Jack Froggart scored a hat-trick at St James' Park on their way to clinching their first title. Such memories would become an unflattering yardstick for those who followed in that famous team's footsteps. There was a real sense of missed opportunity. Back in 1950 the pecking order for the modern game was still wide open – Portsmouth were going places, or so it seemed. Nine years later, the places they were going included long away trips to Rotherham and Scunthorpe. That's because they were relegated to the

Second Division in 1959 after finishing nine points adrift at the bottom of the First Division. Life in the second tier was no walk in the park either. After narrowly avoiding further relegation in 1960, they did go down to the Third Division in 1961. The pendulum would continue to swing in the directions of success and failure, but Portsmouth would never recapture the glory of those two seasons. How could they?

It didn't matter, Pompey were still the team for local lads to support. Any boy playing football in Paulsgrove would have wanted to play for Portsmouth at Fratton Park. Bobby was no different. He too grew up dreaming of playing for them and started playing football at the age of six – as he put it himself, 'When I was in school everybody played, so I just joined in.' George Smith became Portsmouth manager in 1961, getting the club promoted at the first time of asking by winning the Third Division title. It meant local derby games with Southampton in the Second Division for the first time since 1927.

Despite the 34-year wait for a competitive meeting the two sides had met many times during that time in a combination of Hampshire Cup, friendly and war league games organised during the Second World War. But this league fixture brought with it an added edge.

Ron Reynolds was a rare thing – a Southampton player who lived in Portsmouth. A goalkeeper who, having joined from Spurs, moved down from Haslemere to Langstone Harbour in Portsmouth. His son David went to school in Portsmouth and became better known as the son of the Southampton goalkeeper Ron Reynolds. Some of the teachers even called him Ronnie. There was some reason to it – David was a goalkeeper like his father and football helped him settle in to his new surroundings. In terms of distance Haslemere is not far from Portsmouth. On a good day you can take the A3, cruise through the South Downs and be in town in less than 40 minutes. But in terms of the haves and the have nots there was a far wider gulf between the two places. It was an eye-opening experience for David. The standard of education was some way off the one he had left in the leafy surroundings of the Home Counties. The intelligence of some of his new class-mates didn't stem solely from the algebra in the school textbooks. They were smart in other ways, and there was something new and charismatic about some of them to David. They were streetwise.

David began training at Portsmouth, as did Bobby. Some local schools handpicked their best players for weekly coaching sessions at Fratton Park, although David remembers the standard of coaching and facilities being relatively poor. 'Sessions would take place in the cold and wet in a poorly lit area of the Fratton Stand on Thursday nights. Bobby stood out like a sore thumb because of his stature,' said David. 'He was much smaller than a lot of the other lads. Some of them looked like they'd been brought up on a diet of raw meat – they looked a good two or three years older.' It wasn't just his height that David noticed though. 'Bobby was nippy and he had a cheeky-chappy attitude, he reminded me of Tottenham's Tommy Harmer,' he added, referring to the slight but skilful inside-forward who played alongside his dad at White Hart Lane in the 1950s.

Physical strength was one thing, but mental toughness was another equally important factor. 'A reputation as a player could go before you – people might want to bring you down a peg or two, but Bobby was one of those who didn't let that bother him,' said David. 'He had the mental capacity to shrug that off.' David didn't think he was able to do that as well as Bobby. Sometimes, his gut got tied up in knots at the prospect of another trial or a big game. It was debilitating, exhausting even. By the time David was 16 he'd moved back to Haslemere, but he still played against Bobby, this time at a Southampton trial at The Dell, on a dustbowl of a pitch in May. 'I suffered at the hands of Bobby that day,' said David. 'He scored past me – and I probably knew I wasn't cut out for a career as a professional footballer, but Bobby was.'

Bobby had cut his teeth on the playing field of Paulsgrove. The closest thing to being wrapped up in cotton wool was to wear shin pads. Getting good grades at school was all well and good, but you needed to be street-smart to evade the hostile attention of bigger and stronger opposition who took pleasure in demonstrating those very qualities on the field of play. David's experience of life as a developing footballer echoes through the ages. Although always denied by those in positions of power where English football is concerned, it has always seemed there has been a clear mandate for those selecting schoolboy footballers: bigger is better. Every failure by the international team is always followed by a debrief – a report saying never again, that the need for a root and branch approach to how players are developed is needed pronto. But it never lasts. Impatience wins out – the fixation has always been on the here and now. Portsmouth were no different. Their hand may have been forced, but their lack of foresight would cost them a significant player and Bobby his dream of being signed by the team he grew up supporting and the city that dominated his skyline.

5

Just Fish In The Sea

BOBBY had a trial for Portsmouth when he was a teenager. 'My mates impressed them,' said Bobby. 'I didn't.' His whole life had been a journey in sport marked by continual progression until this – the snake after a run of constant ladders. Bobby later reflected on his fate, by saying he was glad the way things eventually turned out. Ron Elsley grew up on the same street as Bobby. The two-year age gap prevented them from exchanging anything other than the odd hello on the way to school, but Ron still knew exactly who Bobby was. By this time Bobby was at Paulsgrove Secondary Modern, where in 1964 he took part in the inter-schools athletics championships – a competition between 14 Portsmouth-based schools. Ron still has the results from the competition. Bobby won the long jump with a distance of 16 feet, also coming third in the triple jump.

He excelled at cricket, proving himself to be a bit of an all-rounder by being the leading run scorer and taking the second highest number of wickets, while his uncle Albie remembered he played a mean game of table tennis.

Despite his other sporting talents Bobby's sights were always set on football.

Maurice Hewlett was a 14-year-old schoolboy from Winchester when he first met Bobby at a Hampshire schoolboys training session in Timsbury in 1964. He'd never heard of Bobby until that point, but, he recalled, 'Within half an hour that was the only name I heard from most people.' Maurice recognised Bobby as someone with plenty of confidence. 'He wasn't that big, but he was quite solid and even at that age he'd frighten people, he wouldn't hold back in a tackle.' Southampton brought a youth team to that training course to play against a select XI from the county hopefuls in order to assess their potential. 'Stokesy played in it,' added Maurice. 'Even though he'd been to The Dell to train with Southampton it didn't stop him charging into the opposition – he was like a little battering ram.'

Southampton were on the lookout while his trial at Fratton Park with Portsmouth would have almost certainly been when Bobby was around 14 in 1965. Portsmouth were feeling the pinch and were looking at what they could do to cut costs. A local businessman, Commander R.B. Cooper, believed a successful team was of great importance to the city. He offered to donate £5,000 to the club if nine other benefactors did the same. Fifty grand would have helped strengthen the squad but with no further donors the deal never materialised. The money was needed, not for players, but to clear their overdraft. Portsmouth were £70,000 in the red. They raised £5,000 by selling their youth hostel. Extra revenue then came in from the weekly pools scheme, which covered the wages. All gate receipt money could be thrown at the overdraft. But they weren't out of the woods – it was necessary to tighten the belt further. Manager George Smith took a long hard look at the situation. How many footballers did a club really need?

Or to be more precise, what was the club getting for the £10,000 a year being paid out on the youth scheme? His answer provided the solution. Cutting costs was simple, he only needed to scrap the reserve and youth teams.

He ran the idea past the club directors. They thought he was out of his mind. Without reserve teams there would be no match practice for the players not in the first team and no chance of giving up-and-coming youngsters an opportunity. And without junior teams and youth coaching schemes how would they uncover local football talent? But they'd missed Smith's point.

It wasn't simply a case of scrapping the reserve and youth teams, it was about drastically reducing the playing staff and costs. He shot the directors' arguments down in flames with a one-liner he became known for. He repeated it in a 1968 interview with the BBC's Kenneth Wolstenholme, who asked Smith why he did not run a youth team at Fratton Park. 'Why should I?' Smith told him. 'There's only fish in the sea around Portsmouth. It's no good kidding yourself that you are Manchester United when you are a struggling small town team with money a rare commodity.'

Bobby had already slipped the net, but Smith was being bullish. Had money not been an option he would have surely maintained the youth and reserve teams. As far as he was concerned it was a luxury they could no longer afford. He saw no evidence it was producing any players worth keeping. With money freed up they could cut their overheads and money would be available to buy players ready for first team action as and when they were needed. Today the term 'small town team' is used as a term to belittle others. Smith wasn't being disparaging, he was merely referring to the size of the city and the money the football club had available. The club couldn't cash in on its heritage and silverware. He believed too many clubs had tried to keep up with the higher wages the best teams were able to pay.

Being deemed not good enough for your local team was one thing, but Bobby was now part of a generation that weren't even worth having a youth team to aspire to. It was a kick in the teeth for teenage boys who had pinned their hopes on wearing the blue shirt. The cost-cutting measures might have saved Portsmouth's skin, but at what cost? The circumstances created a quirk of history that reverberates to this day. Their incompetence in recognising talent had the knock-on effect of Southampton winning the FA Cup.

It was also wrong. Within a year of that interview Bobby was playing for England's under-18 team. However you want to dress it up, Portsmouth overlooked Bobby, who went on to score their rivals' most famous goal. Quite simply the club's scouting network had let them down. Someone on their patch who would have run through a brick wall for the club had been judged and the jury said no thanks.

Scouting is an area that has continued to fail the club over the years. Steve Mills and Malcolm Waldron were from Gosport and Havant respectively, and both served Southampton well. More recently, Alex Oxlade-Chamberlain and James Ward-Prowse have both played for Southampton rather than their home team. Ward-Prowse's family are avid Portsmouth fans. As a boy he trained for both teams before his parents recognised that Southampton were better equipped to develop his gift.

One swallow might not make a summer but would £10,000 of investment on one player not have been worth it if that player were able to display all the attributes Smith was looking for? The more he talked about what he looked for in a player, the more he seemed to be describing the very attributes Bobby showed as a young player for Southampton. With only 16 players in the entire

Portsmouth squad, everyone was trained to be versatile so that he could cover more than one role, and every player was fired with what Smith called the 'I love Portsmouth' feeling.

In many ways, Smith's methods worked. They gave the club some form of stability. Smith didn't believe the removal of the maximum wage was the source of clubs' financial troubles, it was their own reckless overspending that was the problem. He felt far too many clubs had tried to keep up with the likes of Manchester United and had found themselves trying to cope with paying high wages which consequently pushed themselves further into debt. In other ways he was stuck hopelessly in the past. Discipline was everything to him. He couldn't stand the new fashion for long hair – as far as he was concerned men should have a short back and sides. No doubt the forthcoming trends of the 1970s would have been difficult for him to stomach. Worse than long hair were slackers. Pulling your weight was not entirely sufficient, he wanted his players to show devotion to the football club. Players who fell short of his standards were shipped out, replacements brought in with the money gained.

But perhaps Smith's biggest bugbear was moaning, or to be more precise, players who whinged about not having the rub of the green. Having once heard one of his players blame defeat on not enjoying the run of the ball, he took the players out on to the training ground and asked them to look at the ball he put on the grass. His point was that the ball won't run for anyone unless somebody kicks it. In Smith's mind luck didn't exist. Nor did shades of grey – the world was black and white. Other than the hair he would later grow over his ears, Bobby was exactly the sort of player and personality that Smith was after. He was local, too. As a hard-working player with a good command of the basics and an eye for goal he could well have become the poster boy for the club during what was a difficult time.

George Smith's cutback vision became reality – Portsmouth went into pre-season training in 1965 with 16 players. That was enough to have a substitute. The lack of reserve football didn't mean a holiday for the four unselected players – they would be expected to muck in, too. If they weren't taken to the game as spectators they faced the prospect of being sent to scout future opposition. Smith's sergeant major style of management suited the situation Portsmouth were in, but he wasn't everyone's cup of tea. He was known to sometimes criticise players heavily when an arm around the shoulder may have done more good. With the squad being so thin he was naturally unsympathetic about injuries. Many players were playing with injuries.

The streamlining of the playing staff allowed for more time for personalised training, but Smith's training methods weren't flexible enough to accommodate different players' needs. Everybody had to do the same training, irrespective of a player's fitness. The work involved circuit and weight training and even one-a-side games of football and exercises designed to improve the fighting aggression of players. Then there was something called the gallows, which was reported to have been designed by the players. It was designed to improve their heading ability. It involved two footballs which were suspended and were able to be adjusted to any height. All this training took place before lunch with players reporting back for eight-a-side practice games.

Smith joked that with only 16 players he should have kept them in a greenhouse. Not that he had any mind for preservation – as far as he was concerned his player were going to be in shape or be broken. The latter proved to be true when coach Gordon Neave chipped a bone in his right arm during training. He continued to supervise training in a plaster cast, highlighting the precarious situation the club was in. Neave had been a Portsmouth player during the glory years of the late 1940s and early 1950s and was rumoured to have been spotted by a Portsmouth scout while on National Service in Egypt. It was another kick in the teeth for Bobby and for Portsmouth. There they were, able to recognise talent on some sun-scorched field in a different continent more than 2,000 miles away, but they couldn't spot what was under their nose in the shape of Bobby.

Was Bobby's size a problem? David Reynolds's memories were of big, strong young men playing in Portsmouth. As a former sergeant major in the Royal Artillery was that the attribute that Smith was naturally drawn towards? It's unlikely it will ever be known. The slashing of the squad paid off – Portsmouth consolidated their position in the Second Division with a mid-table finish. It was the season that Southampton were promoted. By then Bobby was an apprentice at The Dell. His schooling had taken a back seat. Those who excelled in their eleven plus were sent to Portsmouth Technical College in a blazer. Those who didn't remained on the estate at Paulsgrove Secondary Modern. Opportunity still existed though, both in and out of the classroom.

Mark Newman went to Paulsgrove Secondary Modern with Bobby. 'We played all sports: football, rugby, cricket and tennis – teachers made themselves available on week nights and Saturdays so we could play sport,' said Mark, who along with Bobby was part of the school's tennis team. Bobby was captain. 'We used to play against other schools on our tarmac playground.' Mark still has a photograph of the school tennis team. They are sat in two rows, their white school buttoned shirts tucked into their white PE shorts. Their choice of footwear remained true to their roots. 'We didn't have any designer trainers either – we wore white plimsolls and our football socks,' added Mark.

Tennis in Paulsgrove – three words that the outside world would have thought have no business together in a sentence. Like the council sign in the park in Leominster Road prohibiting golf, local residents remain naturally suspicious of any pastime that requires the wielding of an instrument.

In England, tennis remains best known by Wimbledon – a fortnight in summer when bored television cameramen spend the time in between points zooming in on a growing throng of wealthy celebrities, as if to hammer home the thinly concealed ownership of the game belonging to those who have, rather than those who have not. The tournament, despite all its pretensions of glamour and sophistications has all the sexiness of a church fete. But in Paulsgrove during the 1960s it was just another game that was played and enjoyed.

Mark's memories of Bobby at school centre on an incident away from the sports field. It was the school leavers' assembly, which took place in front of the whole school. Each pupil was called in turn to shake hands with the headmaster and presented with a pocket-sized copy of the New Testament. The headmaster took this opportunity to make a public showing of Bobby. He couldn't leave Bobby's decision to go into football pass without comment. Bobby stood and listened as his headmaster told him he was making a mistake. Mark winces at the thought. 'The headmaster was right, but for the wrong reasons,' he said. 'It wasn't the time or the place to say that to Bobby.'

It was a different time. Working-class school leavers weren't the lost cause some strands of media will have you believe today. Most pupils had futures lined up in secure apprenticeships. Mark went on to work as a BT engineer for 42 years – he also had two back-up apprenticeships in case that work ever fell through, as a fitter and turner and with Southern Electric.

Bobby had no back-up plan, although Mark remembers him being in the top classes at school. Mark often thought that his headmaster's point could have been better made at another time and more discreet place. It's quite possible it had been. Bobby had this ability to deflect. Trying to penetrate his laid-back nature often proved difficult, not that it put his headmaster off. He saw it as his duty to do the right thing, even if it was unpopular. You get the impression he'd spoken to Bobby about this before. His concerns were obvious – pinning all your hopes on a footballing career with no back-up plan seemed like a risky strategy. It wasn't that football was no good, but not having a safety net in place was unnecessarily foolhardy.

Bobby waited for his headmaster to finish dispensing his career advice, then he accepted his handshake before leaving the stage looking embarrassed and a little sheepish. So Bobby left school with all of his eggs in one basket. His dad was insistent that he followed his brother in getting a trade, but Bobby had no interest in doing so. He could draw well. He could also cook. Helen Harris would often return home and wonder what the smell was coming from the kitchen. 'Albie can't cook,' she said. 'But there was Rob stood at my cooker making Albie some lunch.' In Bobby's mind he had no need for a trade. Albie believed his nephew's future lay in football, 'He only ever had one thing in his head. He wanted it bad and I made sure he got it.'

6

Secret Saint

IF Bobby's dad had his way, Bobby would never have set foot in Southampton at all. As former Southampton full-back Bob McCarthy recalls, 'Bobby was Pompey through and through. He put his heart and soul into everything – if he was in your team he'd run all day for you, but he was probably disappointed to not have been signed by Portsmouth.'

Portsmouth hadn't wanted Bobby, Southampton had though. David Stokes's attitude had nothing whatsoever to do with any football-related prejudice between the two rival clubs. Frankly, he didn't care for the game his two sons devoted so much time to, he simply wanted Bobby to gain steady employment and in his eyes football seemed anything but. When Bobby's performances for the school team in Paulsgrove caught the eye of Southampton scouts he confided in his uncle Albie. 'Well what do you want to do, do you want me to take you to the trial?' asked Albie. Bobby's dad didn't drive, Albie did, so he drove his nephew to Southampton for the trial, deciding it was best to keep it a secret from Bobby's dad.

Albie wasn't motivated by the vicarious pleasure of seeing his own footballing dreams fulfilled by a younger relation. He just wanted what was right for Bobby, because when it came to the game itself he felt the same as his brother-in-law. 'I can't abide football, I hate it – I wouldn't go to the bottom of my garden to watch a game,' said Albie. 'But I think everyone should be able to do what they want to do in life.' There was a time when many thought Bobby's older brother David was the better footballer. At six feet-plus, David was much taller than Bobby and scored plenty of headed goals. But he decided against pursuing a football career, taking up an apprenticeship as a toolmaker instead.

Tom Parker was waiting for Bobby in Southampton on the day of the trial, making sure Albie's travel expenses were reimbursed. 'He would put a fiver or a tenner in my pocket every time I took Bobby to Southampton,' said Albie. 'Then he asked me if I thought Rob was good enough to be a footballer.' Albie believed he was. Although Bobby was only having a trial for an apprenticeship with Southampton, Albie firmly believed he could make a professional career from the game.

Could Bobby not just have told his dad he wanted to be a footballer? Albie shook his head, 'No, his dad would have gone crazy.' Of course, Bobby's plans couldn't be kept secret from David forever. 'How his dad ever found out I don't know,' said Albie, who was confronted when Bobby's dad said to him, 'You took him to those trials, didn't you?' The exchanges that followed pitted David Stokes's dogged pragmatism against Albie Harris's rugged idealism. 'Yeah, I went behind his back,' said Albie, 'but you only go through this life once and the boy drove me up the wall to play football, it's what he wanted to do with his life.'

Tom Parker asked Bobby back for another trial, after which he was offered an apprenticeship. This required his parents to give their consent by signing the registration papers, which gave Albie a bit of a problem. Bobby's parents hadn't thawed on the subject of their son's future. 'Well, that's that, I thought,' laughed Albie, who decided to tell Bobby's dad straight. 'He's playing football whether you like it or not,' he said. 'I'll carry on taking Rob to Southampton because he's going to be a footballer.'

'No he ain't.'

'Yes, he is.'

'No he ain't.'

'Just come and sign the bloody papers, David,' pleaded Albie.

David Stokes wouldn't back down – nor would Albie, 'I told him he couldn't live his son's life for him. He needed to let Rob do what he wanted to do, but he was so insistent about him going to do a trade.'

'But then he was so proud of him,' said Helen.

'Oh yeah,' said Albie, 'but only afterwards.'

It was left to Bobby's mum to finally convince David that maybe Albie was right. So Albie drove Bobby and his parents to Southampton where Bobby was signed as an apprentice at The Dell in 1966. It would never have happened without his uncle Albie.

Bobby's potential was spotted by Tom Parker, who was scouting on behalf of Southampton manager Ted Bates. Pigeonholing Tom as a scout does him a disservice. Although if there was a competition of all-time great Southampton scouts, Tom has a pretty strong case for being named the champion of all time. He did two things in his career that had enormous repercussions for the fortunes of the football club. He was Southampton manager in the 1930s, when he brought Norwich City striker Ted Bates to the club. Then in the 60s, having been brought back to the club as a scout by Ted Bates – who was by this time manager – he recommended the club signed Bobby. Ted and Bobby made very different, but hugely significant contributions to the history of Southampton. Neither of them were from the city, but Tom – the man responsible for bringing them to the club – was born and bred in Woolston, long before the bridge was built over the River Itchen to the city and St. Mary's Stadium. Despite attempts to gentrify Woolston in recent years it remains a very much working-class suburb of the city and no amount of coffee houses or newly-built waterfront-facing apartment blocks is likely to change that anytime soon. Any town planner who wants to find out where it's at should see how they get on ordering a rum daiquiri at the nearby Obelisk Hotel, The Bridge, or The Swan. Sophistication begins and ends with a lager top – Bobby would have approved.

But Tom was more than just a kingmaker – he had a playing career of his own and it was more successful than both Bobby's and Ted's. It began with nearly 250 games for Southampton, before he was eventually prised away by Herbert Chapman's Arsenal, where he made a further significant contribution, becoming captain and leading the London club to their first FA Cup Final victory in 1930. Tom was getting on for 70 when Bobby signed as a schoolboy in 1966. Southampton had been promoted to the English First Division for the first time in their 81 years. When teams get promoted to the Premier League these days one of the first things people ask is how they are going to stay up. The implication is that their only hope is extreme caution. This caution often involves not playing younger players because their inexperience represents risk to survival in the big league dependent on parking the bus in front of their goal and hoping the odd counter attack can nick enough wins to avoid relegation.

But defensive play was never on the agenda at The Dell in the 1960s. It was good news for an attacking player like Bobby. Southampton supporters could stomach losing.

What they were far less keen on was their team not regularly visiting their opponents' goalmouth. The star of the team was Terry Paine, part of England's 1966 World Cup-winning squad. He appreciated the fans wanted to see attacking football. 'Back then Bobby fitted into what the Southampton way was about. It wasn't about not losing, it was having a go and trying to score goals,' said Terry.

Their first season in the top flight was marked by an incredible amount of goals. Only four teams scored more than their 74 goals, although nobody conceded more than the 92 they let in. They finished the 1966/67 season two places and four points above the relegation zone. They narrowly avoided relegation again in 1968. Jimmy Gabriel expands on Terry's thoughts about the Southampton supporters. He joined the club in 1967, although his initial experiences of The Dell were as an Everton player. 'I had the chance to see the tremendous support the Southampton fans passed on to their team. Even though we beat them that day, their fans cheered them on from start to finish and I thought that was fantastic,' said Jimmy. So, no shortage of entertainment and all during a time when defenders could throw their full weight around, as former Southampton left-back Denis Hollywood will testify. He highlights a teenage Bobby's physical condition and sunny personality. 'He was very fit – always out the front in training runs. Not fantastic ability, but he made up for that in work. He had a real willingness to work for the team,' said Denis. 'He was very bubbly and always joking.'

The Southampton team was filled with established names and strong characters. Fools were not suffered either on or off the field. Bobby would be excused for keeping his own counsel, or being shy in their company. He was neither according to Denis, 'No, he always had an answer.' A footballing education on the municipal fields of Portsmouth had taught Bobby well, which was just as well with players like Denis, who remembers Bobby being unfazed by the established names. Like Denis, John McGrath had a tough guy reputation on the pitch. 'Several of the players were invited back to a hotel room during a pre-season tour to a fellow guest's room who was a snake charmer,' said Denis. 'John was scared stiff of snakes, and the bloke tells us not to make any sudden movements in case we disturb the snake, then Bobby comes in with his beer and goes "boo" – it frightened John to death.'

Denis too found himself on the wrong end of one of Bobby's pranks. 'For away games we used to leave our cars at The Dell and meet at 1pm at Southampton Central Station. I'd just bought a big white mac. It was very fashionable at the time – not that the other lads thought so,' said Denis, who'd hung his new coat up in the carriage. Having been through a tunnel Denis couldn't find it. Bobby had let it out the window of the fast moving train. 'Tommy Jenkins told me it had billowed in the wind like a sail,' said Denis. The coat was returned to Denis the following week by a British Rail worker who was also a Southampton fan and had seen what had happened. Denis wasn't cross with Bobby. It was the sort of mischief that took place. On the field or the training pitch was another matter, liberties were not taken without consequences.

In person, Denis is softly spoken and polite – everything his reputation on the football field was not. Stood in his south coast home, Denis thumbs through his copy of *All the Saints* – a book published by Hagiology Publishing, who specialise in books on the club's history. The book features every player who has played for the club in the years between 1887 and 2013; as well as being an exhaustive and unrivalled club document, it also doubles up as a very adequate door stop.

The book features Bobby and Denis's old friend Tommy Jenkins, who now lives in the US. Denis had planned to send the book to him as a gift. He's since thought better of it. At the time it seemed like a good idea to get some of his fellow ex-Saints to sign it for Tommy. In hindsight it might not have been the best idea to do so while at a supporters' function where alcohol was heavily involved. 'Look at that,' said Denis, opening the inside cover and shaking his head. 'I can't send it to him now.' He points to two hand-written messages from Jim Steele and Mark Dennis, both inscribed in blue biro. The messages, although very much personal and from the heart, weren't quite the choice of words Denis had in mind.

This considerate side to Denis's character tells very little of the more physical environment in games that his no-nonsense approach was often responsible for. But what would Denis do if the opposition's winger nutmegged him? Sat on the sofa in his cosy lounge, Denis edges forward, kills the volume on his TV and slips into a slightly stronger strain of Glaswegian. 'When I played you could tackle, right?' said Denis. 'And you could tackle from behind. If the winger had the ball you could go through him.' Denis always saw himself as more of a midfielder, but with a defensive crisis on Ted Bates's hands he was forced to play in a more defensive position. 'I was a ball winner and I was quick. Ted Bates was struggling for full-backs in the early 1960s and he ended up putting me in that position.' He laughs at the task faced by defenders today, in an age when the laws of the game are far less lenient on the methods they were once able to use. 'They've got no chance these days.' Bobby may have turned Denis's coat into a kite, but he wouldn't dare show him up in training.

Although the defenders Bobby was up against had reputations, attacking players in 1966 were more than a bunch of wall flowers forever getting sand kicked in their faces by bully-boy defenders. The tough tackling went both ways. Denis remembers playing against Manchester

City's Mike Summerbee. 'He hated me,' recalls Denis. 'When we played he'd approach me and say something like, "Get your pads on you little bastard." A little bit of intimidation went a long way. If you clatter the winger you've got half a chance. Tommy Jenkins played in front of me in those days. If their full-back was giving him a hard time I'd say let me hammer him.'

The trick was simple. The winger would let the accused go past him in time for an oncoming defender to body check the onrushing player. These kind of tactics would be used in training, too. Southampton had their own attacking players who could look after themselves though. Terry Paine didn't rack up over 800 games for Southampton by being nice. He was invited to open Southampton's new multi-million pound training ground in recent years. The state-of-the-art facilities are a far cry from what the club used back then. 'Sometimes we trained in the car park. We'd put our plimsolls on and move the cars before we got started,' said Terry, who insists there was no pecking order at the club.

While it was rumoured Bobby and a few of the other apprentices would help Terry in replying to his ever-growing collection of fan mail, he believes his England caps weren't leverage to call the shots. Many would disagree. Terry once helped out with the youth team. Bobby thanked him. 'He was one of the nice people,' said Terry. 'He'd come through the system, like many of us had. There was mutual respect for that.' It became clear that this respect did not constitute going soft on young players.

'Breaking into the team took patience and time,' said Bob McCarthy, a full-back who made his first team debut in 1967, but had to wait three years until he was a regular. Bob felt ready every day of those three years, but being good enough wasn't enough to make the breakthrough, you had to be better than the first-teamers to become a regular starter in the first XI. 'Local players who'd worked their way through the "A" and reserve teams didn't always get the chances they should have,' said Bob. 'You were often used as back-up.' Bob put Bobby in that category – he had to slug it out every day in training to be in with a shot. And slugging it out came with its own occupational hazard.

'You had players like Cliff Huxford around back then,' recalls Bob. Huxford was a man whose thighs made Stuart Pearce's legs look like vegetarian toothpicks and took games on the training pitch every bit as seriously as on Saturday afternoon. Making a fool of him was to have a death wish. 'When I was a young lad George O'Brien once threatened to floor me during a training game,' added Bob. 'Everyone was keen – there's always that rivalry between the established players who are trying to keep their places from young lads sniffing around.' It could be an intimidating environment for younger players, but an accepted one. It was also an aspirational one. As well as the first and reserve teams, the club had an 'A' and a 'B' team that played in the Hampshire League. They too wore the red and white striped Southampton shirt, but it was a somewhat faded version. Playing for effectively the fourth team meant they were using hand-me-downs. But the 'B' team were amateurs. The door was still open to progress through the ranks, but Bobby was signed as an apprentice. After impressing in the 'A' team he went up into the reserves.

It wasn't just the younger players who lived with uncertainty. The older and more experienced Southampton players felt it too. They would limber up in training by jogging around the perimeter of the pitch at The Dell, muttering to one another about the prospects of some of the younger players at the club. There'd be a few grunts and then maybe someone would spit before the inevitable curtain raiser, 'What about so and so? He's been scoring plenty for the reserves.'

The question would be weighed up and then fronted out. 'Him? What's the point of being able to run like a train if you're always shooting over the Archers Road stand?' They'd laugh and nod. There was safety in numbers, but there was insecurity, too. A young man's progress could mean the end of the road for the older professional, and then what? A CV as a professional footballer didn't mean a thing when it came to finding work in the outside world. And while that day would inevitably come, for the moment, while jogging around the pitch on a weekday morning, it could be hidden away in the back of the mind.

But it never really went away. There was always a new wave of players – working their way up through the 'A' and reserve teams. Bobby was one of them. Many of these younger players had an entirely different point of view – it was the older players who were standing in their way. Bob McCarthy had grown up supporting Saints while captaining the various age groups of Southampton schoolboy teams before finally signing for the club as an apprentice on the same day as Mick Channon did. Terry Paine once presented him with a trophy at a local awards ceremony, now they were team-mates.

Not everyone could make the grade as a professional footballer, although that wasn't to belittle the achievement of holding down a regular place in the reserves. 'Just to put on the Southampton schools shirt was the best thing since sliced bread,' said Bob. 'Then you'd be looking at breaking into the "A" team, then if you made the reserves you'd be thinking "bloody hell" – it was the biggest thing in your life. But breaking into the first team was the dream.'

Once the dream became reality it was hard to go back. 'Reserve football was a good standard, sometimes we'd get a few thousand watching,' said Roger Fry, another local lad and full-back. 'But there's nothing like playing first team football and once you've experienced it reserve team football didn't come close.' He remembers spending lunchtimes in the nearby Fitzhugh pub between morning and afternoon training sessions. Although there was a drinking culture at the club, Roger and Bobby were there for lunch rather than a pint. As was Ray Ames, another young apprentice. Although he has since passed away, a few years ago he spoke to David Bull, Terry Paine's biographer, about what life was like coming through the ranks with Bobby at The Dell with Southampton in the First Division. 'I was a bit overawed,' admitted Ray. 'I remember thinking, "What am I doing here?"' But there he and Bobby were, training alongside the first team that included England's Terry Paine.

Terry was rarely injured, despite being an attacking player during a time when defenders could hack away at attacking players. Very few did so successfully to Terry Paine, though; not as far as Ray remembered. 'No one ever caught him – not while I was there,' said Ray. 'I remember when Terry went into midfield when Jimmy Melia had a cartilage operation. They moved Terry there because he could spray the ball about. We played a game between the first team and the reserves. It was one of his first playing in midfield.' Ted Bates wanted to get Terry used to the physical attention the position carried, so he used Ray and Bobby. To the outside world, Paine was the big cheese at the club, fresh from being part of England's triumphant World Cup-winning squad. Bobby and Ray were given specific instructions to rough up their star player. Ames came off worse than Bobby. 'Ted said to me and Stokesy, "Just sit with Terry. Wherever Terry goes, don't let him get the ball. Just stop him from playing." That's all we had to do,' said Ray.

It sounds simple enough. 'I remember tackling him and I ran away with the ball. He tried to hack me down. I stumbled on and he hacked me down again and I went sprawling. By the time I got up, there were three or four reserve-team players grabbing hold of him. I think because we were youngsters Terry thought he could take advantage of us because we were nippers and we wouldn't have done anything about it.' A bit of rough-house tactics wouldn't have been new to either Bobby or Ray – not having come this far through the ranks. But coming from Terry Paine, Southampton's star player – fresh from being part of England's World Cup squad, with his dark Elvis Presley quiff and that familiar ridge of Victorian English teeth – it's only natural they'd be taken aback and drawn into their shells. Mollycoddling was no good for youngsters. If they wanted to be professional footballers they'd have to mix it with the best, and that's what Terry Paine was.

Jimmy Gabriel believes the young players at the club got an invaluable education from training alongside Terry Paine. Like many, Gabriel felt Paine was a brilliant winger. 'He could make great dribbles and crosses to set up chances for his team-mates and could also score goals,' said Jimmy. 'In practice Terry played as good as he did in games and the younger players would watch him dribbling, crossing and shooting as well as anyone in the game.' Although a respected professional, Gabriel was more avuncular than some of his other senior colleagues. He used a pat on the back rather than a knuckle sandwich in order to get the attention of the younger players. 'If Bobby or any other young players were messing around during practice I would tell him that training is like a ladder that helps us to climb to the top of the soccer mountain,' said Jimmy. 'Bobby used to listen.'

Jimmy used another motivational ploy that could have easily been misconstrued as patronising at best if carried out in the wrong way. But it worked with Bobby. Having won the league and FA Cup with Everton, he would bring the medals to training for the youngsters to see. 'I wanted to lift their standard of play,' explained Jimmy. 'Once they'd seen the medals I could see them walk away determined to win at least one of them in their career.' Bobby would remember that experience. For a long time it was the only FA Cup winner's medal he'd ever seen. There would be a time when he too would want to share his medal. Like Jimmy Gabriel, Bobby's gesture wasn't born out of the desire to boast, but rather to give pleasure to others; others who, unlike Bobby, would never be in a position to experience glory on such a scale.

7

Breakthrough

ON Easter Monday 1969 the playing surface at The Dell bore the evidence of the previous eight months of football played on it. The pitch was hard. Down through the middle grass had given way to patches of dusty earth. Mick Channon was firing blanks, so Southampton manager Ted Bates gave 18-year-old Bobby his chance in the first team. Southampton put five goals past Burnley and Bobby scored two of them in front of a 20,000 crowd. England manager Alf Ramsey was among them. He wouldn't have come specifically to see Bobby but he would leave Southampton knowing who he was. Everyone there did. Bobby left the field breathless, heading for the tunnel only able to utter a few words: it was 'wonderful' and he was 'delighted'. If Southampton kept this form up there was still the chance of qualifying for European football.

Less than a fortnight later the *Southern Daily Echo* ran a story about the man Bobby had replaced in the side wanting out of the club. For a moment, Bobby's breakthrough looked as though it meant the end for the club's all-time leading goalscorer, and perhaps if not the greatest ever player then certainly one of them, long before he had established himself as either. Mick Channon had been out of sorts, so Ted Bates took him out of the firing line. He responded by handing in a transfer request to leave the club. It was not accepted. Bates wasn't hanging him out to dry, he simply recognised it was the right time for him to rediscover his form out of the glare of the first team. He spent the remaining few weeks of the season playing for the reserves.

As far as the experienced professionals at the club were concerned, if any of the crop of young players at The Dell in 1969 was going to make it big then the smart money was on Mick Judd. Southampton-born, Judd turned professional when Bobby was still an apprentice. As he recalls, 'If you could afford to pay 50 pence you could get an apprentice to clean your boots.' Bobby would end up cleaning many pairs. There aren't many Southampton players who can say they scored in a 3-0 win over Arsenal at Highbury, but Judd is one. He was one of several in the reserves with serious designs on the first team. With only one substitute allowed it could be a frustrating experience, with around 30 players in the squad competing for 12 places up for grabs on a Saturday afternoon. Mick's cross set Bobby up for his first career goal. 'I said to him before the game, "Let's get you a goal,"' said Mick, who played with Bobby many times for the reserves. 'Bobby used to run to the back post then dart into the near post – he made that run a lot, we used to score goals for fun in the reserves. So that's what we did. I drove the ball in at the near post and Bobby headed it in.'

The Dell was busier than Bobby was used to. The team sometimes trained there, while the reserves would often play there; but when they did the concrete terraces were mostly empty. The noise of players communicating in short shouted commands of 'man on' and 'time' reverb-erated around the concrete stands of the ground. Not against Burnley. Bobby could have been forgiven for being a nervous wreck in the build-up to the game. Reason composed him as much as it unpacked his achievement into its merest components. In his mind there was no great secret to his two goals, he was simply in the right place at the right time, choosing not to mention that this in itself, the nose for goal, is a very specific skill.

His humble nature went a step further still, revealing an even more unusual attitude in the world of professional sport. When talking about how he found out he'd be making his debut he put the feelings and careers of others ahead of his own. 'My first feeling was one of disappointment and I couldn't look at Mike [Channon] – I just didn't know what to say,' said Bobby, who realised he was replacing his friend. Phrases like hard luck never sprung to mind.

Ask Mick Channon almost 50 years later about getting dropped back in the late 1960s and he'll own up to not really remembering, 'When you're a kid you're in and out the side,' said Mick. Like Bobby, Mick scored in his first game, a draw at home to Bristol City three years earlier as the club closed in on reaching the First Division. Bobby could hold it together. He was no bag of nerves. He demonstrated how once the news he was replacing Channon had sunk in he was able to use common sense to overcome any pre-match jitters. 'Then the excitement bubbled to the surface. Strangely enough I wasn't very nervous for I felt if I played well everything would be okay, but that if I didn't, then it would be put down to the fact it was my first game.' Many have the talent, but not everyone is able to deal with the nerves that come with playing in front of crowds. Bobby's way of dealing with it made perfect logical sense; but for many, logic goes out of the window when the nerves creep in. When common sense gives way to anxiety the power of reason is useless compared to a constant seat on the toilet.

Bobby's debut was hard earned and something to remember, but not something to bask in the glory of for too long. Not if he wanted to stay there. Doing so required resilience. It also required some degree of luck. Mick Judd had none of that. His professional footballing career ended at the age of 22, quickly slipping away from people's consciousness. This was from no fault of his own – he tore a cruciate ligament after colliding with the opposition goalkeeper having scored for the reserves. The days of reconstructive knee surgery remained in the distant future. Knee surgery was a far cruder procedure – comebacks from such injuries were unlikely. So despite several attempts to return to the game, Judd was forced to retire having played 14 first team games.

By 1970, Mick Channon was getting picked for the England under-23 side while Judd was playing for Mitchell in the Southampton Junior League. Judd still loved the game but the knee was unable to stand up to it. Even while playing local football he admitted he had to compromise, backing down in certain 50-50 challenges to avoid further aggravating his knee injury. Judd went on to have a successful business career. But as Bob McCarthy says, the roll of the dice plays its part. 'Mick Channon had so much confidence. Right from the age of 15 you just knew he was going to go through and become a professional. He never really got an injury either – that helps to sustain a career in the game.' Bobby would suffer the inevitable injuries most footballers suffer, but nothing to threaten his career.

He scored again a few weeks after his debut against a Manchester City side who would have been forgiven for having one eye on the FA Cup Final they would go on to beat Leicester City in. Although Southampton lost to Spurs on the final day of the season, it didn't matter. By finishing seventh the club had qualified for European football for the first time and Bobby had made a significant contribution. Southampton had taken advantage of a loophole in the qualifying rules for the Inter-Cities Fairs Cup, which is now known as the Europa League. Only one club from each city was permitted to enter the tournament. Chelsea and Arsenal finished above Southampton, but Spurs finished higher than both, so it was they who went on to represent the capital in the competition.

Bobby was young but he'd already played abroad for the England youth team. He'd been through the various trials up at Lilleshall, as a large group of players were whittled down to the final squad. Plenty didn't make it. Jimmy Neighbour went on to play more than 300 games for Spurs, Norwich City and West Ham; but he wasn't selected. Nor was Alan Hudson; best known as the playmaker in Chelsea's 1970 FA Cup Final-winning team.

The news would arrive in the post, a letter informing you whether or not you'd been selected. The Football Association were the men in blazers. Their attitude and customs were still pretty old fashioned, whereby in their paperwork Bobby was referred to as R.W. Stokes, in reference to his full name Robert William Thomas Stokes. It made Bobby sound more like a Test match batsman than a footballer. The formal nature belied the crusty stance of the FA. Neil Rioch was a centre-half with Luton Town while he was part of that England team. For home games they stayed at the Lancaster Gate Hotel, which was near the Football Association headquarters. Sir Alf Ramsey came to visit, shaking the boys' hands and giving them titbits of advice.

Bobby was part of the side that beat Belgium home and away to qualify for what was essentially the European Championships. It meant travelling to East Germany for the tournament in May 1969, during the height of the Cold War. 'There was nothing for the players to do,' said Neil. 'It was quite common to see soldiers on the street with machine guns. Some of the lads wanted to go home. I questioned how much they wanted to win.' The East German hosts brushed them aside – England were out. It was Bobby's last taste of international football, but still further evidence that Portsmouth had dropped a clanger in not signing him up.

Where memories are thin a photograph remains. It belongs to Keith Eccleshare, who although naturally proud of representing England, confesses to remembering little about that time – it was so long ago. In the photograph Bobby is sat in the front row in a crestless white England jersey, his Adidas football boots polished to within an inch of their life and he is grinning from ear to ear. For some, this was the pinnacle of their footballing careers – for Bobby it was a further landmark. Southampton had achieved something new and Bobby had become a big part as a teenager. But he'd still have to earn his stripes at the club. The following 1969/70 season was spent in and out of the first team, playing 16 games, scoring two goals. This set the tone for what was to come in the following few years. Breaking into the team was one thing, but with only one substitute allocated to the squad on matchday, staying there on a regular basis was quite another.

8

Morning Train

BRIAN O'Neil heard the same noise every day he arrived at The Dell for training. It was the sound of a football echoing off the walls of the club's gym. Bobby would be inside kicking a ball around by himself. He didn't have a driving licence, so rather than travel by car he caught the early morning train from his home in Portsmouth to Southampton. Under that mop of dark hair, with a paper under his arm, Bobby wouldn't be stopped or noticed during the ten-minute walk from the station up Hill Lane to The Dell. He would have been there for the best part of an hour before anyone else had arrived. 'Every shift was a hard one with Bobby – he'd run his bollocks off and give you everything,' said Brian. 'He might not have been the greatest player, but he used to try bloody hard and by the end of a game he'd be totally knackered. You couldn't always say that about everybody.'

To the average football supporter, the idea all players aren't breaking their necks for the cause is hard to stomach – even if the evidence sometimes suggests otherwise. It's the same when it comes to being able to use both feet.

Bobby was known for being prepared to strike the ball with either foot. This is not a skill those not interested in football would think ranked highly among those whose job it is to kick a ball around for a living, but as those who watch and love the game know, even some of the most talented players have been predominantly one-footed. Many professional footballers go to great lengths to avoid using their lesser foot. Qualities normally taken for granted like accuracy, power and even proper contact, can be found seriously wanting. Brian believes much of Bobby's two-footed ability was honed and maintained in the extra hours spent in Southampton's fairly spartan, wooden-floored gymnasium at The Dell.

Those who saw him play during his four years at The Dell have fond memories of Brian and his unbridled enthusiasm for the game. He continues to live in South-ampton. Dressed in shorts, despite miserable weather, he enjoys a trip down memory lane. So much so that after two hours spent discussing life at The Dell with Bobby in the 1970s he suddenly becomes embarrassed for not offering to make a cup of tea. With his shirt untucked and his football socks forever rolled down to his ankles, very rarely did Brian ever wear shin pads. He was protected from injury by his reputation for being a ball-winning midfielder; as he recalls. 'I had Denis Hollywood playing behind me – if I didn't get the opposition, he would,' said Brian. It was true.

Neither were strangers to hearings at the Football Association's London-based disciplinary committee for receiving three yellow cards in the space of a year. Resulting suspensions would be around six weeks with fines of up to £125 when £100 was a lot of money. Draconian punishments maybe for just three bookings, but these were the days when yellow cards were only dished out to players for decapitating opponents.

What was perhaps most peculiar about Brian is that he didn't ever own a pair of football boots. He much preferred wearing other people's. This wasn't due to any fetish – a new pair were no good to him, he had a preference to wear boots that had already been worn in. At around 5ft 7in he is the same height as Bobby was, and is adamant he would have worn a pair of Bobby's at some time. Not that having the wrong-sized footwear ever stopped Brian from playing. 'I was running late once. It was round a quarter to three and I didn't have any boots,' so Brian ran into the boot room. 'The only pair left belonged to John McGrath.' McGrath was a 6ft tall centre-half. Not only was he taller than Brian, he also had much bigger feet. Unperturbed, Brian put them on for the game with Sheffield United. He could only side-foot the ball or else the boots would fly off his feet. But he still managed to score.

Although born and bred in the north-east, Brian began his career with Burnley. The nature of his move to the south coast in 1970 gives further clues to how the club operated during the time. Brian was taken in Burnley chairman Bob Lord's Rolls-Royce out of town and up to the moors, where another car was waiting for them there. 'A little fella came out.' Brian recognised him. 'It was Ted Bates. The chairman turned to me and said, "Well go on then, have a word with him." Ted said he wanted me to play for Southampton.' Brian warmed to Bates immediately. 'I knew I was safe with him. He was so genuine – he sold Southampton to me right away and asked me if I would come down. I said I'd be down tomorrow – I didn't even ask what the wages were.' Brian hit it off with Bobby straight away, enjoying a lifelong friendship.

'Bobby was likeable, loveable even. He didn't have a bad bone in his body and it was a breeze to be round him; he was lively and he was a great mate,' said Brian. 'When I was poorly – I was in hospital for two months – Bobby came to visit me in the north-east. I didn't want him to go.' Brian smiled, although the memory is not a fond one. His hospitalisation in the early nineties came after being the victim of a vicious attack that left him in a coma. It hasn't affected his sunny outlook on life. Sometimes he'll stop halfway through a sentence about Bobby to laugh. Although the two played in very different positions they had similar and clearly defined hands-on roles in the Southampton team.

The home support at The Dell was important to Brian, 'Southampton always had great fans, either they took to you or they didn't, but they knew we always had a chance at The Dell. We never got beat very often there. It was a fortress. The crowd would help – they were right on top of us,' said Brian. Although demolished for flats in 2001, The Dell remains reminiscent of the traditional British ground. Bobby and Brian appreciated the dynamics of the team back then. 'Without Mick Channon, Ron Davies and Terry Paine we'd have been knackered, but if the rest of us could scrap and Terry could get past his full-back and cross it; well, sometimes I'd run back to the centre circle. I knew if Ron was on the end of it then it was a goal.' Brian looks into space for a moment to reflect on that. 'Nobody could beat Ron Davies in the air, nobody.' Manchester United certainly couldn't – Davies scored all four Southampton goals in a 4-1 win at Old Trafford in 1969.

Brian and Bobby would have been required to scrap and work, something not lost on Terry Paine. 'Bobby was the link between midfield and attack – towards the end of my Southampton career he did a lot of my running,' said Terry. Bobby's fetching and carrying enabled Terry to carry on doing what he did best, crossing in, more often than not, for Ron Davies. Terry is very clear on what Bobby's qualities as a player were. 'The less time he had on the ball the better player he became,' said Terry. 'But, if he dwelled on the ball he wasn't as good in my opinion – he'd make less good choices with his passes. He chipped in with his share of goals, though – and he had good technique, particularly shooting – he was a very clean striker of the ball.'

Having broken through in 1969, consolidating his place in the 1969/70 season with 18 appearances, his progress juddered to a halt during the following 1970/71 season. In November, Bobby was called in to cover for the injured Ron Davies for what was his only start of the season. He wasn't able to finish the game, being helped off of the field shortly before half-time after colliding with Newcastle goalkeeper Ian McFaul. Bobby lay beside the goal. Ted Bates was concerned, telling reporters, 'We were not sure what was wrong with him at first, but it soon became clear that he was in trouble. He's such a tough little boy and certainly wouldn't complain twice if something wasn't the matter.' Ted was right – Bobby had three cracked ribs.

It was a far less pampered time where injuries are concerned. Hugh Fisher broke his leg after colliding with Arsenal goalkeeper Bob Wilson in 1971. 'I knew it was broken straight away,' said Hugh. 'Later on I was lying in a hospital, sweating; I could hear the doctors talking in the distance – they were waiting for a surgeon, he was coming back from his holidays.' The surgeon returned to operate. As far as Hugh is aware it was one of the first operations on a broken leg which used steel pins to reinforce the bones without the need for a plaster cast. The steel pin was driven in from the knee and in two days Hugh was able to do exercises. He went on to play every game the following season.

While these operating techniques were cutting edge, the rehabilitation back at the club remained firmly rooted in the past. 'Jimmy Gallagher was the club physio,' remembered Hugh. 'He was an old-fashioned army guy, a get-on-with-it type, always in his white coat.' Hugh came in hobbling around on his crutches at The Dell, to which Gallagher responded to bellowing, 'Throw them bloody crutches away!' Being injured did not mean getting pampered. Not that players wanted pampering, they were eager to return to action. This probably explains why Bobby was back playing so quickly, doing light training within ten days of cracking ribs. This enthusiasm didn't prevent the injury setting Bobby back.

The rest of the season was either spent with the reserves or as an unused substitute with the first team. Irrespective of injuries it was as though Bobby had hit something of a glass ceiling. He'd yet to fully establish himself, which asked the question whether it was time for him to leave the club for pastures new. Bob McCarthy was very much in the same boat. 'Leaving does cross your mind, but I was Southampton through and through. It was my team. To say I'm going to up sticks and leave,' said Bob, shaking his head. 'Those were the days you didn't have agents, so you were restricted, and couldn't just say you were going to bugger off somewhere else. So it was quite a tough time to break through. Likewise, you had players in front of you. If they had injuries then you got your chance. As a young player you could be used as a scapegoat. Bobby was at The Dell a long time and he broke into the side, but he never really made it as an established player at the club. It was tough times.'

It was left to Brian O'Neil to lighten the mood. By now Brian was living in the Hampshire countryside, where Bobby sometimes stayed. A neighbour's pony grazed on Brian's land. 'We were dressed in our club blazers, but Bobby said he'd always wanted to ride a horse,' said Brian, who wasn't prepared to let a lack of saddle or helmet prevent Bobby from having a horse-riding experience. 'So I put him on and smacked the horse's arse and off it went, flying into the distance.' Bobby was gone what seemed like quite some time. When he returned his blazer was the worse for wear. 'Bobby came back covered in mud and his blazer torn,' laughed Brian. 'He didn't play hell with me though. It was give and take and he was never mad with me.'

Brian goes past what was once The Dell on most days to walk his dog at the nearby common. Very rarely does he do so without thinking of Bobby, 'I laugh of the times we had.' Brian hadn't laughed like he had when remembering Bobby for a long time. The Dell is now a residential area, mostly flats. Brian doesn't see bricks and mortar when he looks at the site of his Southampton playing days, he sees memories of a time long since past spent with a good friend he will never see again.

9

Pinned To The Wall

ALL-TIME leading Southampton goalscorer Mick Channon is very clear when assessing Bobby's style of play against his own. 'Bobby was a conscientious footballer – a great team player,' said Mick. 'I wasn't.' For those who saw him play, Mick encapsulates an era at The Dell when a group of young men a little rough around the edges enjoyed their football as well as their lives off of the field. Life was kept simple: work hard, play hard. The ethos was let's get out there and have a go, try and score some goals – if we get beat then so what, we'll go down the pub and have a drink.

Mick is held in high esteem by fans of the club. When supporters meet him they don't see a man closing in on 70, they see the mutton-chop sideburns that sprouted forth from his cheeks 40 years ago, the carefree attitude, and the windmill arm he'd wind round and round every time he scored a goal. The hair on Mick's head has thinned, but there is a mischievous glint in his eye when he talks about Southampton.

In person, he plays down his achievements as a footballer. Today he is the successful horse trainer that the time he devoted to horses as a player suggested he always could be. Behind his desk in the office of his stables in West Ilsley, Berkshire, is a large framed photograph of him and Alan Ball playing for Southampton. Mick had a long and enduring friendship with Alan Ball. He was also close to Bobby, who would quite often stay over at Mick's in the Hampshire countryside.

Mick is clear on the difference between him and Bobby. 'I was more of an individual player than Bobby,' said Mick. 'I could score goals if I was up front on my own. But Bobby would have been given a specific job to do, which would probably mean he had to defend as well as attack. It was no good asking me to defend and I was never asked to either.' Mick smiled at the notion of him being asked to track back and defend, as if even the idea was laughable, which of course it was. Although both attacking players, he doesn't believe you could compare his style of play with Bobby's. 'He was far more disciplined than I was,' said Mick. But was that really the case? After all, he played regularly for England. 'Oh God, yeah,' added Mick. 'I was given a free role to just go and fucking do what I wanted in what was pretty much a one-nine-one system. The idea was to nick a goal – survive for another year. Bobby was a great, clean striker of the ball. He was a good goalscorer, but he wasn't prolific, but that's because he was given lots of other jobs to do.'

Once again, Mick reiterated that this is not to belittle Bobby. 'He was like a hod carrier; he did all the fetching and carrying. Every team needs them for Christ's sake – Bobby Charlton needed Nobby Stiles in the World Cup Final. In them days that role was commonplace.' Southampton were usually operating on a shoestring budget under Ted Bates. The main aim was often maintaining their First

Division status. Brian O'Neil thinks Bates worked miracles to stave off the threat of relegation. 'The club never had any money,' said Brian. 'But Ted knew what Stokesy was all about.' That graft Bobby was prepared to offer was the minimum requirement.

Among the seasons spent battling relegation, Bobby had a taste of glory as part of the Southampton side that won the national five-a-side championships at Wembley. He was joined by Mick Channon, Jimmy Gabriel, Terry Paine, Brian O'Neil and goalkeeper Eric Martin, who was the hero by saving penalties in the shoot-out victories over Sheffield United, then West Ham in the semi and Leicester City in the final. Bobby's penalty effectively sent them to the final. Eleven-a-side remained a different ball game though. Brian thinks Bobby was a bit unlucky due to the stiff competition for attacking places in the starting XI. Like Bobby, Brian was known for his work rate on the field. 'That was my trademark, if I couldn't give 90 minutes it was a waste of time,' said Brian. But he doesn't put his levels of stamina in the same category as Bobby. 'He was fit as a fiddle – he was always at the front in training runs. If someone would have said to me after a game that I'd worked as hard as Stokesy I'd have been over the moon.'

Hugh Fisher was one of many Scots playing for Ted Bates's Southampton sides. Like Mick Channon, Hugh quickly pinpoints Bobby's lack of self-belief. 'He was a great little lad,' said Hugh. 'And he should have been confident in himself because he was a good player. But I don't think he thought he belonged in the same company as Channon and Osgood.' That was understandable, they were both England internationals. Hugh is adamant that Bobby's work rate during games was higher than anyone else at the club at the time. 'He used to think that he didn't have the ability of Channon,' said Hugh. 'He used to actually talk about it like this in front of us – so he was determined to give everything. He had a big heart and he had no problem facing up with some tough men; he'd stand up to them all.'

It was as if Bobby's hard work was trying to compensate for something. Mick Channon speaks very well of Bobby, but like many from the Southampton sides of the 1970s, he feels Bobby lacked self-belief. Many players have it in spades. Mick had his fair share of moments out of the team as a teenager in the late 1960s, but by the 70s he had established himself not only in Southampton's side, but also England's. 'I don't think Bob believed in himself as much as we believed in him,' said Mick. 'He was important to the team,' Mick hesitates for a moment as he looks for the right phrase, 'but I always felt he thought he was a bit worthless. It's a sad thing to say – I just don't think he realised he was as good as he was.' It's not difficult to see how this could foster a growing sense of insecurity. The not knowing if he'd done enough in the previous game to be selected again the following week.

Perhaps Bobby did lack a bit of confidence, but he wasn't stupid either. Players like Channon and Ron Davies were not going to be dropped if they were fit to play. One was a tall target man, the other a quick lone striker, roles Bobby was not ever right for. His flexibility sometimes became a disadvantage in cementing a first-team place. Mick took a deep breath before offering his thoughts on why this would be the case, 'P'haps because at times he was in and out of the side? I dunno? He was used as a tool of the manager and probably ended up becoming a jack of all trades but a master of none.' His flexibility had become a hindrance to his long-term career prospects.

The process of finding out if he had been picked for the first team became an issue for Bobby. 'The routine was the same every week,' remembers Paul Bennett, another local lad who progressed through the ranks, making over

100 appearances. 'The teamsheets for the first and reserve teams would be pinned to the wall at The Dell every Friday after training,' said Paul. 'That's how you knew who you were playing for on the Saturday. If you'd been dropped you'd get called into the manager's office for a quiet word – told maybe what you didn't do well in certain situations.' Not that there was any time to sulk in the second XI. 'You did that in your own time,' explained Paul. 'There were plenty of others in the "A" and "B" teams who wanted to play for the reserves – you played for pride.'

The teamsheet wasn't such a concern for everybody. Channon could afford a laissez-faire attitude to a piece of A4 paper. He didn't think anything of it. 'It was your team and you probably took it for granted,' suggested Mick. 'Bobby was always floating, always in the squads.' Hugh remembers Mick's laid-back attitude. 'Most of us would be hanging around waiting for the teamsheets to go up, but Mick was off. "See you later, lads," he'd say. We accepted that.' Mick produced the goals, he knew his place was guaranteed.

Bobby would be on edge come Friday. This leads Hugh on to what it takes to deal with the ups and downs of professional sport. 'Not every single pass you make is going to be great,' said Hugh. 'But if you do make a mistake then don't panic about it, get on with the game. That's part and parcel of professional football. But Bobby could get a bit down on himself if he thought he had a bad game.' Hugh stops for a moment, grins and shakes his head. 'He'd be saying to us, "That's it, I won't be playing next week." We used to try and gee him up, tell him to stop worrying, try to give him a boost.'

Not that Bobby was some kind of hopeless waif. Criticism was dished out to players if necessary. 'Back then bollockings happened,' said Terry Paine. 'If a pass was sloppy you got a verbal.' He is sure he would have done that to Bobby over the years. Terry doubts if that's still the case in today's game. 'Too many of them seem so quiet, as though they're worried about upsetting someone, but it was part of our game and all forgotten about after.' Terry doesn't remember Bobby ever answering back on the field, not because he was frightened of the repercussions, but because he channelled his response in a different way, through positive action on the field of play.

This was easier said than done at times of low confidence. Every now and then the BBC likes to showcase footage of Southampton getting walloped 7-0 at Elland Road in 1972. Southampton have had bigger defeats over the years, they had bigger defeats that season, losing 8-0 to Everton. Sadly the television cameras weren't at The Dell when Southampton beat Leeds earlier in the season, but they were there to record the beating against that iconic Leeds side. Roger Fry remembers Bobby running around and chasing shadows like the rest of the team that day at Elland Road. 'It's a horrible feeling to know you've had a nightmare,' said Roger. 'I've seen the game since and I think what was I doing? After the game the changing room was silent and Ted Bates was pacing up and down, putting his finger in the air as if to say something, but no words came out.' Roger did not play for the first team again. Unless you were a superstar a football career could be a world of one-year contracts and insecurity. Roger went on to forge a further professional career at Walsall, while Bobby lived on the edge of the void created by Roger's exit. For those on the fringes the game was not brimming with long-term career opportunities.

Fortunately there was plenty of horseplay to take the edge off the reality of how quickly and easily a career could be finished. Brian O'Neil recalls a night out after a draw at Maine Road to emphasise the silliness the players could get up to. 'A point at Manchester City was great for us – they had a team of greats. We came back to Southampton for a few drinks – Stokesy ended up staying at mine. He was starving and asked me if I had 'owt to eat.' Brian's kitchen cupboards were a little bare, but as ever, he was prepared to improvise. 'I only had a few eggs, a tin of beans, and a tin of PAL – the dog food,' said Brian. 'I mixed it all up in the pan and gave it to him. He ate the lot.' He never told Bobby what the ingredients in the snack were and Bobby never asked.

Anecdotes like this suggest this was a carefree era; and in many ways it was. Bobby was a young man and doing the thing he grew up dreaming of doing for a living, but at times some might have you believe the seventies was nothing more than one long episode of *On The Buses*, with days filled with banter, sexually available women and general bunking off. It wasn't the case. The football club were in for a shock when Ted Bates stepped down as manager in 1973 after 18 years. It blew a hole in everything Bobby knew.

10

Down But
Not Yet Out

BOBBY never played more games in a season than the 47 he featured in during Lawrie McMenemy's first campaign at Southampton, 1973/74. He would only ever experience one other season at The Dell with more goals, finishing as the club's second top-scorer with 13. These personal milestones for Bobby were insignificant compared to what that season ended in, which was relegation. It meant that at the age of 23 Bobby's career as a First Division footballer was over. Relegation still sticks in Lawrie's craw, 'Check our points tally that season,' he said. 'Make sure you put that in.'

Today he is recognised as the club's most successful manager. His achievements continue to cast a tall shadow over every boss the club has had since. He brought silverware, European football and some of the game's biggest names to the club in the following 11 years of his tenure, signing Alan Ball, Kevin Keegan and Peter Shilton, as well as introducing a youth scouting network that later resulted in Alan Shearer and the Wallace brothers joining the club. He also brought his own attacking brand of football to the south coast, at a time when brands were still something you bought at the supermarket. He freely admits that in today's game he probably wouldn't have made it as far as his second season at The Dell after getting relegated in his first. Had that happened the FA Cup may never have found its way into the trophy cabinet.

Second Division football looked highly unlikely at Christmas. Bobby played in the side that beat reigning league champions Liverpool, and was ever present as Southampton went on a ten-game unbeaten run that stretched over nearly two months between September and November. By mid-December they were in fifth place. They were far less anxious times for Bobby in terms of waiting for the teamsheet. The club's form took a turn for the worse in the new year, with only three league wins after Christmas.

Having finished third from bottom, Southampton were the first club to be relegated under the new rules which saw the bottom three, not the bottom two clubs – Norwich City and Manchester United in that season – relegated to the Second Division. It's not simply the issue of relegation that bothers Lawrie – it's the context in which it's often discussed. The suggestion is he was either initially out of his depth at the wheel of a First Division club, or that in his determination to stamp his own authority on the dressing room he tried to change things too quickly. But perhaps what bothers him most of all is the number of points they went down with. They finished on 36 points, one behind Birmingham City. That tally would have been enough to stay up in any of the previous 35 seasons. No team had been relegated with the same high number of points since Manchester City and West Bromwich Albion in 1938.

That season at The Dell remains crystal clear in Lawrie's memory. He was speaking at Potters Heron, a restaurant in the Hampshire countryside, north of both Southampton and the M27. It's a familiar environment for Lawrie. This is the place he announced to an unsuspecting world that Southampton had signed European Footballer of the Year, Kevin Keegan, from Hamburg. Now 35 years later, mid-morning on a weekday he walks undisturbed to a table. The restaurant was sparsely occupied by a handful of businessmen, sat with their laptops open, talking about marketing strategies, seemingly oblivious to the presence of Lawrie, who was smartly dressed in a dark shirt and blazer, while sipping from a cup of tea. The first thing to notice about him is how very tall he is. You can't help but think his physical stature would have been a valuable asset in a profession that boils down to earning the respect of young men. Especially where his first job at The Dell was concerned, which was simply to prove himself. This meant getting to grips with the club.

'Many of the senior players had been at the club a long time – this made my job more difficult, because I had to sort out the dressing room – sort out who was who,' said Lawrie. 'And they were weighing me up, too. Bobby was never going to be a problem though. There were some senior players who weren't supportive, but Bobby was never in that category.'

Ted Bates had tended to turn a blind eye to what went on off the field as long as players gave their all in training and on Saturday afternoons. What went on away from the pitch was often drinking. Lawrie wasn't quite so forgiving – he wanted to bring in more professionalism. He didn't think it was too much to ask for players to arrive for games dressed in a shirt and tie. The notion of getting suited and booted didn't appeal to Mick Channon's feral nature. On recalling his first away trip with the club, Peter Osgood remembers asking Mick where his overnight bag was. Mick was armed only with his toothbrush – as far as he was concerned that's all he needed for a night or two away from home.

In the end, players did begin arriving at games in a shirt and tie. Up until his appointment at The Dell Lawrie had never been up against Bobby before, having worked in the lower divisions at the other end of the country with Grimsby Town and Doncaster Rovers. Lawrie began to bring his own players in. Peter Osgood and Mel Blyth signed for Southampton, but continued to live in London, giving Bobby company on the short trips to The Dell from Southampton Central station. Mel Blyth is the first to admit he wasn't always in the best of moods by the time he'd tackled another morning's travel on British Rail and arrived at Southampton, 'In professional football there's not always much nice going around, but Bobby was nice. He'd do anything for you – nothing was too much,' said Mel. 'I'd leave the house at six in the morning to get the train down. Some days I'd get off the train saying "fuck this" and "fuck that". Then Bobby would appear. He'd have got me and Ossie tea and toast from the station café. He did that every single day.'

Lawrie was very aware of what the other players thought of Bobby. 'He was loved by all the players – he was never a confident, cocky sort of player, but the senior players respected his ability. He had that shyness about him, which looking back was probably a lack of confidence. He looked around at the big names like Mick Channon and thought I'm not as good as them – they're international footballers,' said Lawrie. 'But they would have been the first to tell you that every team is made up of a blend. He was an integral part of that team – all good teams are made up of road sweepers and violinists.' In Lawrie's book, Bobby was a road sweeper. This is not a criticism of Bobby's ability. If you ask him if road sweepers play as an important a role as violinists – the players with free roles – the answer is emphatic. 'Without a doubt,' added Lawrie. 'A team of violinists never won anything on a football pitch. They're waiting for the likes of Bobby to work their socks off, to set them up – Ossie often benefited from Bobby's play. He was a nuisance to defenders. If he lost the ball he'd snap back at their heels to win it back.'

Peter Osgood would go through the motions of that routine, but not with anything like the same intensity as Bobby, whose arms would be pumping as he gave chase, applying pressure in the hope the opposing defender would be forced into a mistake, maybe put the ball out of play, or not find his man with his pass. But even if he did, Bobby would continue to grind down the opposition. Bobby could be relied upon to give his all, even if that sometimes meant falling short of what might have been required.

Lawrie offers further thoughts on why Bobby was popular with the other players, 'Aside from his 100 per cent effort he was good company, he wasn't a big head – he had a nice nature. But he didn't have that streak in him.' That streak Lawrie refers to is what separates the great from the good. When people talk about the greatest player to have ever played then it's unusual for Pelé's name not to crop up. All sorts of hyperbole has been written about him over the years, but when things got nasty he could dance – he wasn't shy of dishing out a right hook or two. Not that *this* streak is only about having a nasty side, it's about being able to explode and own the moment through a latent combination of talent and self-belief. 'That possibly held him back a bit. Great players have that and they can turn it on at any given time,' added Lawrie. 'Bobby didn't and that was the difference between him and the step up to the next level. But he changed my life and the players' lives too.'

Self-belief plays a huge part in being a professional footballer. Hugh Fisher believes very few have that inner confidence right away, they have to develop it. 'Some players need around 50 games under their belt before they feel settled as a professional,' said Hugh, who puts himself in that category.

In his long career he can name just three players who he thought were super confident in their abilities right away as teenagers: Alan Ball – who Hugh shared digs with, alongside Emlyn Hughes, at Blackpool; Mick Channon, and Steve Williams, whose emergence at The Dell in the late 1970s spelt the end of Hugh's professional career. 'They were super confident of their own ability from the age of 17 or 18,' said Hugh. 'Bobby never had that in his make-up.'

Of course, it's a chicken and egg scenario, ability fuels confidence and vice versa. Peter Osgood was the first big name Lawrie bought to the club and he wasn't going to tell his new signing how to suck eggs.

'International players don't need coaching,' explained Lawrie. 'The lower down the leagues you go the more coaching you have to do – the higher you go the less you do. Players like Alan Ball don't need coaching, but they need managing.' Man management was probably Lawrie's greatest strength. While he was trying to stamp his authority on the club, he also knew when to cut his players some slack. Jim Steele recalls one incident where his manager did just that, 'Lawrie wanted the players back in the afternoon for another training session – Mick wasn't very keen on the idea. He said, we can't do that gaffer, we've got tickets to the races.' Jim was glad Mick suggested the idea. 'If me or Bobby had mentioned it we'd be told to get on our bikes, but Mick was the ringleader in those days. So we didn't train that afternoon – we went to Fontwell races.'

The spirit of work hard, play hard still ran through the players' veins. Mick and Jim were joined at the races by Bobby Stokes and Brian O'Neil. 'Bobby and Brian put a tenner each on one horse – I can't remember the odds, but they stood to win quite a few quid if she came in, and ten pounds was a lot more money in 1974 than it is now. Their horse went out way ahead, maybe even ten lengths out front. Then, right at the very last jump the horse blows it. Me and Mick were in hysterics, but the other two boys were distraught. They were just stood there, gawping at the last jump. They were both moaning their heads off, then Brian told us he could've jumped that last hurdle, with Bobby chipping in agreeing with him. So me and Mick told them to prove it. They did. The idiots scampered under the barriers – and they're not the tallest – and jumped through the gaps in the fence.' That fence was mostly made up of pretty dense and uncompromising foliage, so there was only going to be one winner when Bobby and Brian decided to tackle it head on; as Jim says, 'When they got back they were all cut and muddy.'

Brian, too, remembers it well, 'The pair of us were covered in shit.' But the good times off the pitch weren't being matched on it. Bobby breathed life into an FA Cup run, scoring in a 3-3 draw with Bolton, then bagging both unanswered Southampton goals in the replay at Burnden Park. The cup run was brought to an abrupt end in the fifth round at home to Third Division Wrexham. They had to wait until mid-March for the second league win of 1974, which came at home to Leicester City. The win looked unlikely as Leicester and England goalkeeper Peter Shilton demonstrated why he was the country's best with a series of impressive saves. The general observation going into this game was where were the Southampton goals going to come from if Mick Channon didn't come up with the goods? Bobby stepped up to the plate, beating Shilton's resistance by smashing one past him from the edge of the penalty area. Bobby was throwing his hat into the ring as the go-to guy to get the club out of trouble, and his goal looked like providing the momentum needed to take into the rest of the season.

The following home game with Birmingham was the opportunity to continue that momentum. Lawrie made his position clear, the players would have to bring their 'A' game. It didn't happen. Hugh believes this was the killer blow. 'We were hopeless that day,' he said. 'The pressure got to us. We could feel and hear the crowd with every bad pass.' The 2-0 defeat was the sign of things to come, failing to win any of the following seven games. Southampton went to Everton on the final day of the season knowing they had to win while hoping other results went in their favour if they were to avoid relegation. Although he was included in the programme notes, Bobby wasn't selected to travel to Goodison Park. Nor was Terry Paine, who had played his last of his 700-odd games for the club. Brian O'Neil was another who'd not been selected, but a sickness bug meant he was called up at late notice. Brian describes another element of the idiosyncratic nature of the club, at the time. He had been looking after Gumbles – Mick Channon's pregnant Basset hound. Gumbles had eight puppies while the Southampton team travelled north.

'When I arrived in Liverpool all Mick wanted to know was how Gumbles was. How many puppies had she had?' said Brian. He remembers that he had one of the puppies, Mick had one and Bobby had one. 'Bobby called his puppy Spock,' said Brian, on account of being a fan of *Star Trek*. Mick's concern for his dog didn't hinder his performance: Southampton beat Everton 3-0. 'We thought we'd done enough,' said Hugh. 'We were waiting on results.' There was the predictable pandemonium after the final whistle. Bobby would have had to make do listening in on the radio at home. Players did likewise, congregating around transistor radios waiting to hear confirmation of the results – Birmingham had held their nerve to beat Norwich City; so, eight years after gaining promotion to the First Division Southampton were relegated back down again. Brian O'Neil scored in the Everton win. By that point he was 30. He, along with Terry Paine, was moved on after relegation.

Southampton had an unremarkable following season in the Second Division, finishing in 13th place. There were glimpses of brilliance. Bobby scored in a 5-0 thrashing of that season's First Division champions Derby County. Their inconsistency was no better illustrated than in their 1-0 defeat in the next round to Third Division Colchester United.

By 1975 Bobby was available on a free transfer. Portsmouth came calling. For the second time in his life he fell through the net of his boyhood team. Bobby was in talks to join his home-town club shortly before Christmas in what would have been a swap deal for Pompey's Paul Went.

By now the club were managed by ex-Liverpool striker Ian St John. It was not to be a happy time for Ian on the pitch at Fratton Park, but he speaks highly of his time on the south coast. When asked about Portsmouth's money troubles back in the 1970s, he laughs that famous Basil Brush laugh and says, 'When have Portsmouth not had money troubles?' Before accepting the position at Fratton Park, he called his old Liverpool manager Bill Shankly. 'Shanks had no hesitation and strongly recommended I go to Fratton Park,' said Ian. 'He remembered the great title-winning Pompey teams.' Ian was relieved of his duties on the south coast two years later. He took up the subject of his Portsmouth tenure with Shankly years later, 'I said, hey, I took your advice and look where it got me and

Shanks says to me, "Sorry son, never knew the difficulties they were having."'

Portsmouth needed players. They could only get them on free transfers and loans. Ian brought Dave Kemp to the club. 'He was genuine and great to work with,' said Ian. 'I felt that Bobby was the same. I'd seen him play a number of times and sensed he was a genuine boy, the kind we were after. If there was money available I would have paid for him to come to the club.' So what exactly was Ian looking for in a player? 'It was a personality thing – we needed players who were prepared to work and scrap. Without that you cannot get results.' The deal fizzled out, with Bobby not able to agree personal terms. He would later offer his thoughts on why the move fell through – he felt Portsmouth might get relegated to the Third Division. It wasn't hard to see why – Portsmouth were struggling hard. Having beaten Leyton Orient in August they'd embarked on a miserable 20-game winless streak, including nine defeats in a row. The writing was very much on the wall.

With half of the season still to go it didn't say much for what Bobby felt he could do for them. But it was astute judgement. Pompey were bottom of the table at Christmas. They stayed there, meaning the league champions 26 years prior were relegated to the Third Division. So Bobby stayed at The Dell. More than 40 years later Southampton supporters remain grateful for that. Big things still awaited him – Southampton were about to go on a famous cup run.

11

Barn Door

SLOGGING his guts out wasn't the only thing Bobby was respected for. He had a good eye for goal; Mick Channon vouched for that. This particular ability fell by the wayside in the two months leading up to the 1976 FA Cup Final. To put it simply, Bobby couldn't hit the proverbial barn door from ten paces – but it wasn't through a lack of trying. 'Bob was a very good finisher – he was underestimated,' said Mick. 'But he was having a minging run – a terrible run, and he hadn't scored for ages. Everyone at the club kept saying, Bobby will scream one in soon enough. We all knew what he was capable of.'

Bobby's finishing prowess wasn't limited to striking the ball, he had finesse. His goal at the Baseball Ground in a 2-2 draw against Brian Clough's Derby County in 1971 said a lot about Bobby, who ran on to a slide-rule pass by Terry Paine and chipped over the onrushing goalkeeper before gently jogging back to the halfway line with no more urgency than had he been crossing the road on his way to the shops for a packet of cigarettes. There were no cupped ears as an ironic gesture to the silenced home fans,

100

or furious pointing to the name on the back of his shirt, just a few handshakes and a little grin.

Having scored against Orient in late February he had to wait two months for another. It was the only goal of the game against Hull City, the week before the FA Cup Final. The focus of the newspaper reports on the game wasn't on Bobby's winning goal though, it was his inability to score more. There was no media vendetta against him – they too had their eye on the big game the following Saturday – it was just impossible for them not to report on the number of chances Bobby missed in that single game alone. On another day he could have had a hat-trick.

Southampton's route to the FA Cup Final began with a 1-1 draw at home to Aston Villa on the third day of January, weeks after Bobby's free transfer to Portsmouth had fallen through. He remained on the transfer list. If another club wanted him they needed only contact the club to begin discussing personal terms with the player. It was a strange quirk of fate that Bobby, who had never been a prolific goalscorer, due to the role he was so often given, had the opportunity to be exactly that in 1976 with the goalscoring opportunities that continued to fall his way during the latter stages of the season. Lawrie McMenemy remembers this very well. 'Chances galore came Bobby's way between the FA Cup semi and the final – he missed so many. I remember pulling his leg about it, telling him he was going to score one eventually.'

It was evident that Bobby had a serious case of the yips. There was a strong argument to suggest that his uncertain future at the club was the root cause of his symptoms of anxiety. If this was the case then it was inevitable that it was creating doubts in his mind. These doubts would take hold of him at inopportune moments, revealing themselves in the split-second decision-making process when he came into view of the whites of the opposition's goalposts. With

Bobby struggling to score the big question was could the team carry someone who was shooting blanks? Was this the time to for Lawrie McMenemy to take him to one side and tell him to get his act together?

'Oh no, no – you don't do that,' insisted Lawrie. 'A manager's job is to build confidence; I mean if anybody's getting a bit too big for their boots then management is about levelling them off if needs be. You just need to work out if the individual is the sort you can do that to in front of the group, because he might crumble. The other option is taking them to one side. Many a time you'd say can you pop into the office after training for a one to one.' From then on in it would be the chance to have a gentle word, not to threaten, but to discuss the situation privately so as to nip it in the bud. But Bobby's case wasn't related to discipline, it wasn't performance either – the effort was still there, he just had a mental block when it came to putting the ball in the net. Lawrie wouldn't criticise him, he'd try and chivvy him up.

'I'd never show him up in front of the others – it was different with Peter Osgood and Mick Channon,' said Lawrie; the latter Lawrie remembers as being a bit snappy when he first joined as manager. 'I had to win Mick over – he'd been there a long time, whereas I brought Ossie in – which makes a bit of a difference. Say if Ossie missed an open goal in training, you could have a right go at him about it. But it'd be like water off a duck's back. You wouldn't do the same with Bobby. Mick and Ossie's attitude would be, "Don't worry, you wait until Saturday." They had that in-built confidence of international footballers.'

Today, the average first team squad is more than double the size of the ones managers had at their disposal in the 1970s. Seeing as Bobby was on the transfer list and not exactly pulling up trees it seemed logical for the club to stop treading on eggshells and pro-actively seek other employment for him. Maybe make a few calls, see what interest they could drum up in the transfer market. But as Jim Steele points out, although Bobby wasn't scoring, he was still bringing something to the team, specifically when it came to helping the strikers. 'Mick was quick,' said Jim. 'And Ossie was strong – if you put the ball up to his head or chest he could hold it, but Bobby linked the two up.'

The two needed him in order to be the players they could be. Bobby was their foil, as he had been for previous Southampton teams. Mick Channon used the phrase 'hod carrier' to describe Bobby's work-rate. As mentioned earlier, Lawrie McMenemy uses a more familiar line to the ears of Southampton fans when he names the two distinct archetypes within his squads at The Dell over the years. 'Any good team is made up of road sweepers and violinists,' said Lawrie, referring to the workers of the team, and the stars and the artists whose abilities meant they were indulged. Both are needed though. 'A team of violinists never won anything on the football pitch,' added Lawrie. 'They're waiting for the road sweepers to do the work, to set them up.'

On his day Bobby could play a mean concerto, but in the larger scheme of things he was very much a road sweeper. This is what held down his place in the team. Despite being on the transfer list and missing a succession of goalscoring chances in the lead-up to the FA Cup Final, his place in the Southampton side wasn't under threat. He was able to do something nobody else in the squad was able to do – the ferreting about to allow Mick Channon and Peter Osgood the necessary time and space to demonstrate their inherent gifts as footballers. So Bobby was ever present in the cup run; he played in both third round ties with Aston Villa, scoring in the 3-1 fourth round win against Blackpool, before scoring a vital equaliser in the fifth round away to West Bromwich Albion. A virus had been going around the Southampton squad, and Bobby was one of several players who played that day feeling very much under the weather. That goal forced a replay at The Dell and Southampton coasted to a 4-0 win. This was no time to lose your place, not with the possibility of making history.

Paul Bennett suffered that fate. He was a local lad. Pulling on the Southampton shirt meant as much to him as anyone. Lawrie McMenemy still feels sorry for him – he wishes he was able to name more than one substitute in the final. Paul was there on the bench at Wembley, with another local, Pat Earles. Both were kitted up but it was nothing more than a token gesture. Irrespective of any injuries anyone in the starting line-up might suffer, they would not be permitted to play any part. Paul had played in the quarter-final against Bradford at Valley Parade. 'It was perfect for him,' said Lawrie. 'It was a bloody hard game – they played up and under and Paul was strong and dealt with it.' He was covering for Mel Blyth, who had established himself ahead of Paul in the pecking order. He had conducted himself well, but luck played its part – the club had someone else, who was deemed superior.

The semi-final draw became an event in itself. Southampton were delighted to have been paired up against Crystal Palace. Their Third Division status meant they were the lowest-ranked team left in the competition. By the same token, Palace were also pleased. Having seen off Chelsea in the quarter-finals their confidence was sky high. Buoyed further by the equally confident and fedora-wearing Malcolm Allinson, they would rather have taken their chances with Southampton than face up to the two other teams left in the competition – defending league champions Derby County and Manchester United.

Southampton's game with Palace was scheduled to be played at Stamford Bridge while Derby would take on

Manchester United at Hillsborough. This caused United manager Tommy Docherty to make his own observations on the two ties, when he said that 1976 would be the first time the cup final would be played at Hillsborough, because as far as he was concerned the other semi-final was a bit of a joke. Docherty was something of a maverick, speaking in the kind of one-liners most people would only have the courage to use at closing time at the pub. As far as United were concerned he was the right man at the right time. The club had suffered the indignity of relegation two years earlier so they needed someone who could handle being measured up against the success of the club's fairly recent past. And although he could be accused of arrogance at times it was rarely without a dash of humour.

Southampton's belief they could win the cup was more understated. Lawrie McMenemy was not interested in competing for headlines with Docherty. Publicly, he tried to play things down, rather than ramp them up. Southampton beat Palace 2-0 in the semi-final with a penalty by left-back David Peach and a rasping long-ranger by Paul Gilchrist, which had it been scored by a more famous player might have been shown every night for a week on the news. Mick Channon later joked that Gilchrist's shot just brushed his sock on its way to goal. For a team who hadn't been in an FA Cup Final for 74 years and had never won it, it was almost impossible to not look ahead towards the final itself. But there were plenty of fixtures between the semi-final and the big day to keep the mind occupied.

Lawrie McMenemy's job was trying to get the team to focus on the league after the semi. 'That was my main task, as I still felt we had a bit of a chance of promotion,' he said. 'And if you look at our record between the semi and the final I think our results showed that we kept working at it, while Manchester United may have taken their foot off the pedal, maybe going to a few functions.' The history books demonstrate this. United's form after their 2-0 semi-final win against Derby was patchy, losing three of their five games, away to Leicester City and Ipswich Town and at home to Stoke City. Southampton's form was better, winning five of their remaining seven league games. They didn't have the luxury of spending too much time celebrating their semi-final win as three days later they had a game at Fratton Park. Portsmouth gave a good account of themselves but Mick Channon's last-minute winner effectively sent Portsmouth down to the Third Division. However, back-to-back defeats to Plymouth Argyle and Bristol Rovers in the lead-up to Wembley were enough for the neutral to predict that Manchester United would be able to take care of Southampton without too much trouble in the final.

If the experts were to be believed it was going to be one-way traffic. Bobby Charlton couldn't be accused of sitting on the fence. He was one of the BBC's studio guests at Wembley and his verdict was that it would be just that; he could see Southampton on the wrong end of a big Manchester United scoreline. This wasn't the prediction of a fool – Charlton was England's heroic World Cup winner and all-time leading goalscorer – a man who'd seen and done it all for club and country. But his ability to score goals from long range with the ferocity of a bazooka seemed to be offset by an inability to properly assess the potential outcome a game of football. Southampton were clearly underdogs, but they were not cannon fodder either.

Charlton could be forgiven for getting a little carried away – he has long been United through and through. But beneath the solemn, earnest tones in his voice lies an emotional man, who at that time had not long stopped playing for the club. Emotion and the occasion itself appeared to have gotten the better of him; it seemed contagious at Old Trafford. United were back in the First Division after getting relegated with Southampton in 1974. They were a young team full of swagger who finished third in the top flight in 1976, and brushed aside defending First Division champions Derby County in the FA Cup semi-final. They were the favourites and rightly so.

Not that Mick Channon could believe the longs odds being given on Southampton winning. He telephoned Lawrie, asking him if he'd seen – you couldn't get anything lower than 5-1 on Southampton winning. Not being a betting man, Lawrie asked if that was a problem. Those odds? In a two-horse race? It didn't seem right to Mick, but it suited him fine – the underdog tag took some pressure off of Southampton. Of course, they didn't want to lose, but they weren't expected to win, even though they still had plenty of good players. These players weren't able to perform consistently well enough to win promotion from the Second Division. Many of them had experienced the big occasion though – so they weren't going to be the proverbial rabbits in the headlights. Mick Channon was an England regular, while Jim McCalliog, Peter Osgood and Peter Rodrigues had all played in previous Wembley cup finals.

Not everyone backed United to walk it. Bobby Charlton's older brother Jack saw it differently as part of ITV's panel of experts. He considered Mick Channon one of the best forward runners in the game, somebody who could catch United out on the counter attack. England manager Don Revie seemed to carry a torch for Southampton. The interest stemmed from his fondness of Lawrie McMenemy. When Ted Bates stepped down as Southampton manager in 1974, club chairman George Reader telephoned Revie for advice. He had no hesitation in recommending McMenemy, remembering the impression he made a decade earlier when he took his Bishop Auckland side to play Revie's Leeds United second XI.

Docherty claimed that he didn't study the opposition. If he did he'd have noticed Bobby was getting himself in great positions, he just hadn't been scoring, but that goal against Hull set him up nicely for Wembley. Southampton made all the right noises about focusing on the league, but the FA Cup Final dominated the horizon from the moment they left the field at Stamford Bridge. It was the same for United. After their semi-final win over Derby, United's Gordon Hill, when asked about the forthcoming final, was reported to have asked who Southampton were. He was to find out soon enough.

12

Southampton Go Mad

YES, he had seen Bobby as a young boy knock a ball about in the garden at home and at the park, but David Stokes had never watched his son play football professionally before the 1976 FA Cup Final. The only time he'd been to Southampton was when his brother-in-law Albie Harris drove him there from Paulsgrove to sign Bobby's apprenticeship papers ten years beforehand. So he went to Wembley to watch his son play, not just for the first, but the only time.

With kick-off fast approaching, Bobby stood in line with his Southampton team-mates on the Wembley turf, working a wad of gum around his jaw as he waited to shake hands with the Duke of Edinburgh. The formalities were nearly over and Manchester United goalkeeper Alex Stepney had sensed a problem with his team-mates that threatened to give the initiative to Southampton. As the oldest and most experienced player in the Manchester

United side, he wondered if some of their swagger was in danger of veering into complacency. 'I remember being on the pitch before the game in our cup final suits,' said Alex. 'It's a fantastic occasion, but I was looking at the Southampton lads, thinking, hang on – yes, they're Second Division, but they've got plenty of good, experienced players. We'd been playing well up until that point, but that counts for nothing in a one-off cup final. I was telling our lads that it wouldn't be easy. I kept reminding them that if we don't perform we'll get turned over.'

Back home in Paulsgrove, Maria wore the red-and-white-striped Southampton jersey Bobby had on in the semi-final. When the game started she turned to her mum, Helen Harris, and asked what the final score would be. Helen didn't sit on the fence, 'Well, I did say it was going to be 2-0, but I also said Rob was going to score.' Southampton appeared to have the focus to match Helen's prediction. Paul Gilchrist was relaxed going into the game. 'It's so strange,' he said. 'It feels like I can remember almost every minute of the match.' Paul, along with all of Southampton's younger and less experienced players, was told by captain Peter Rodrigues to make sure they soaked in the atmosphere and experience of the day. 'I did and I loved it,' added Paul.

What sticks in his mind is the stark contrast of Manchester United's famous red jerseys with Southampton's changed strip of yellow and blue. Having lost the toss to decide which team would wear their home colours, Southampton wore their away kit. They'd worn yellow earlier in the competition but this shirt was brand new for the final. The low v-neck collar created the illusion it was a yellow sweater worn over a royal blue polo shirt.

Bobby followed his captain's advice, quietly taking in his surroundings. Television commentator Martin Tyler had travelled on the bus with Southampton en route to

Wembley, later interviewing Bobby on the pitch while both teams were still in their suits. He kicked off the interview by telling Bobby he thought he was a bit quiet on the bus. Tyler would have been taken aback if Bobby had channelled his inner Muhammad Ali by using the build-up as an opportunity to manifest his personality on the event, but as far as opening gambits go it put Bobby on the back foot. The implication was that Bobby's quiet nature belied a personality which lacked the passion to leave Wembley with a winner's medal. So what might have appeared to be an innocuous question required Bobby to reply with an explanation rather than an answer. Bobby was clear: it was his first time at Wembley, he was simply doing what he could to avoid letting the experience pass him by. His lack of conversation wasn't the behaviour of a man retreating into his own shell due to nerves caused by the big occasion. How he behaved on the bus is what would more commonly be referred to today as focus on the job in hand.

Not everyone in the Southampton dressing room was as laid back. Mick Channon remained an England regular, despite sticking with Southampton in the Second Division. Both the semi-final and the final itself were watershed moments for him perhaps more than anyone else. Although a winner, Mick wasn't crippled by the fear of not winning, he was motivated by a sheer love of playing the game. These two games were something of a dichotomy for him. While they were an obvious high point in his career he confessed that they were also perhaps two of the worst games of his life. Up until this day, Southampton hadn't been able to offer Mick the opportunity of winning silverware. The club gave him almost total freedom on the pitch instead. With Bobby plugging away in the engine room, Mick was able to fully express himself going forward. Now, for the first time in his career it was more important to win than anything. This seemed to cramp his style. It was, however, Mick who had set the tone. Sat in the bath at Stamford Bridge after the semi-final win over Crystal Palace, he was adamant that he wasn't interested in a sight-seeing trip, 'No point getting to Wembley and bloody losing,' he said. 'We've got to go and win the bloody thing.'

Southampton goalkeeper Ian Turner was suffering from nerves on the day. Like many goalkeepers of that era, he did not wear gloves. With the long sleeves of his green goalkeeping jersey pulled up past his elbows, he looked more like a plumber who'd fled the scene of a burst water pipe rather than a goalkeeper about to play in the most prestigious game of the English domestic season. A few years earlier he was playing for Grimsby Town's reserves in front of no more than a few hundred people and now this. The FA Cup Final still had the potential to create scenarios where lesser-known players could become heroes. Gordon Hill had been earmarked as United's main man by Ted Bates's scouting trips, but like Turner, he too had recently risen from the lower leagues, beginning the season with Millwall in the Third Division.

United started the game in a hurry, their supporters raising their voices in expectation every time they began an attack. As predicted, Southampton had to call on their defensive abilities during the first 25 minutes, with United attacking them down the flanks at speed. Much like Bobby and Paul Gilchrist, Nick Holmes was another hard-working cog in Southampton's side. Southampton born and bred, and quiet too, there was a feeling among some of the experts that Manchester United's bravado could extinguish any self-belief the Saints had. This wasn't so. 'We were under too much pressure to worry,' said Nick. 'We got battered in the first 20 minutes and the only kick I got was booting Steve Coppell – I doubt Bobby saw much of the ball in that time.' He didn't. In the absence of possession Bobby showed he had the temperament for the big stage. On the few occasions he received the ball he played the simple pass into the feet of a team-mate to maintain possession, rather than trying to force the game with something unnecessarily elaborate.

Lawrie McMenemy had been instrumental in getting his players mentally prepared for the game. 'The gaffer was very good at reinforcing to us just how experienced our team was,' said Nick. 'He'd actually reel off the number of games some of our players had played compared to some of their players, like Brian Greenhoff and even their captain Martin Buchan.' Lawrie saw that lack of Manchester United experience as a question mark over their ability to handle the big stage. 'Jim Steele, Ian Turner and Peter Rodrigues were brilliant for us,' added Nick. 'Many teams start off well in games, but if they don't score during that spell they can run out of ideas – we got ourselves in the game.'

Having scored twice in the semi-final, Gordon Hill could have been forgiven for taking a look at his opposite number Peter Rodrigues and thinking Christmas had come early. What with his tally-ho moustache, receding hairline and greying temples, 32-year-old Rodrigues looked ancient in comparison and destined to spend the afternoon chasing after the number on Hill's back as he raced away from him towards Southampton's goal. Rodrigues's appearance bore no resemblance to what he was capable of. He got touch-tight with Hill very early on, producing a man-marking performance which helped Southampton weather that early and forecasted storm. For all United's intent, it was Southampton who had the best opportunity of the first half. Like Rodrigues, Jim McCalliog had experienced defeat in the FA Cup Final. He showed a keen appetite to avenge that, often seen looking for the ball, on one occasion running across the pitch with both arms held high above his head, demanding a short square pass into his path. Once in possession, he split United's defence with a through ball to Mick Channon. With Stepney quickly off his line, Channon met the pass inside the penalty area with a shot he guided with the side of his foot. Stepney saved it. Channon should have scored. He walked away from the penalty area with his chest heaving. With his pallid complexion and bushy side-burns, Channon seemed to resemble the decade itself more than any of the 22 men on the field that day. The missed opportunity was as ominous as it was prophetic; if he couldn't score for Southampton, who could?

Although not a substitute, Paul Bennett took his place on the Southampton bench with club coach, former player and all-round stalwart Bill Ellerington. 'With ten minutes left Bill and I were anticipating extra time,' said Paul, who was weighing up the long walk to the Wembley changing rooms to fetch refreshments for his colleagues.

Soft drinks wouldn't be necessary. Helen Harris's hunch was coming to pass, 'As the time went on and it got towards the end Maria looked at me and it went in didn't it.' By 'it', Helen meant Bobby's goal, which came in the 83rd minute, ending an 11-second sequence of play beginning with goalkeeper Turner. It was preceded by Jimmy Greenhoff's speculative long-range strike for United, which bounced harmlessly over a Woolworths advertising hoarding behind Turner's goal. Turner then gave his goal kick an almighty boot, causing the ball to hang for an unusually long time in the air. It momentarily disappeared from the television screen as though its descent had been delayed due to a collision with a pigeon. It gathered so much height that Paul Gilchrist and his marker Lou Macari seemed to have misjudged the flight of the ball, both jumping to contest it in the air a split second too early. Paul's slight flick-on up the field seemed reliant on his mop of curled, dark hair.

The ball reached Channon who, with his back to goal, squared it to his right into the path of Jim McCalliog. Bobby and McCalliog were very much tuned into the same frequency. McCalliog knew United's back four would come out rather than dropping off deeper and as soon as Bobby saw the ball arriving in front of his team-mate he accelerated into the space behind Brian Greenhoff – he knew McCalliog's ability to play an accurate pass. Having already looked to see Bobby's forward run, McCalliog side-footed the bouncing ball with a measured pass over Greenhoff's head. The direction and weight were close enough to perfection.

Having been two yards behind the United centre-back, Bobby was half a yard ahead of him when the ball was played into his path. Greenhoff never recovered. Under normal circumstances, the United defence would have had the opportunity to atone for their positional error and make a last-ditch tackle. But Bobby's first-time shot did not allow them that.

For a moment it looked as though Bobby's run was made too early as he waited a split-second for the ball to drop in front of him. United's last hope, goalkeeper Alex Stepney, had weighed up the situation as soon as McCalliog played the pass through to Bobby. 'It looked like he was going to be one-on-one against me,' said Stepney. 'But I'm ready, I'm set. I knew where he was going to put the ball when it sat up on his left – he's going to go across me.'

Stepney dived to his left. Bobby was certain of the outcome, 'As soon as I let go with my left foot I knew Stepney wouldn't be able to stop it.' He was right. The ball ran across Stepney's body and up against the old Wembley goal's thin green stanchions. David Coleman's commentary for the BBC was to the point when he said that Southampton were going mad. Manchester United did, too, but for different reasons.

Although the disappointment of the day has since cooled, United captain Martin Buchan still doubts the legitimacy of Bobby's goal, 'We looked across in vain for the linesman's flag,' he said. 'But I am convinced to this day that Bobby was offside.' He maintains a sense of humour about it when he says, 'I always joke with Alex Stepney whenever I see him that although Bobby gets further and further offside every time I see a replay, he [Alex] gets down slower and slower on the re-run.' The implication, although only made in a jocular manner, is that perhaps his goalkeeper could have got down a bit quicker.

From Stepney's point of view he actually dived to save Bobby's strike too soon. He was a veteran of more than 600 games throughout his goalkeeping career. That vast experience had programmed his reflexes to expect a powerful strike. 'In my anticipation I've gone down too early,' said Stepney. 'I could see the ball on my way down – it was bobbling in the corner, the bounce of it beat me.' To Stepney it was the perfect mis-hit. The way in which Stepney slips into the present tense when describing the goal, 40 years after the event, emphasises how important the game was to him. Here was a man who had won almost everything in the game with United – the European Cup at Wembley in 1968, alongside Bobby Charlton and George Best – and the league title the year beforehand. The FA Cup was the other major honour missing from his trophy cabinet and time was running out for him to win it.

The most enduring photography of the big moment is arguably of Stepney. Taken from behind the goal, several pictures show him diving to his left, turning his head over his left shoulder as the ball passes his outstretched fingers to reveal a stoic, if not doomed expression on his face. Stepney was the elder statesman among several younger

United players, many of whom referred to him as Steptoe, the miserable older character in the classic British sitcom *Steptoe and Son*. Although his hair was fairly long and in keeping with the time, Stepney's was not in the style of Led Zeppelin or Boston; maintained with a rigid side parting, it was far more akin a brigadier at the turn of the 19th century. Replace his green goalkeeping jersey with a red tunic and stick a white pith helmet on his head and he'd look the part alongside Stanley Baker and Michael Caine in the war film *Zulu*.

If Martin Buchan is bitter then he hides it well. In conversation he remains philosophical about the game. 'It was no disgrace to lose to Southampton, they had some excellent players in their line-up. Everyone knew about Mick Channon and Peter Osgood, but Peter Rodrigues was also a very experienced professional and a good leader, and on the day Bobby Stokes was a little terrier, with plenty of pace,' said Martin, who regrets the absence of a second camera angle on the goal, which could have proved once and for all whether Bobby was onside or not, although, as he says, 'It would have been scant consolation as the goal would still have stood.' Bobby felt he'd mistimed his forward run. However, his interpretation of the television replay differed from Martin's. 'I thought I was offside when the ball reached me,' he said. 'But having seen the replay on television, I realised United had played me onside, so I'm glad I didn't stop.'

Martin had played alongside Jim McCalliog during the latter's spell at Old Trafford. Prior to Bobby's goal, McCalliog had played some dangerous first-time through balls which had split United's defence open. On another day it would have resulted in Mick Channon scoring. McCalliog's growing influence in midfield did not affect United's defensive positioning though. They were not inclined to drop off a few extras yards in fear of Southampton getting in behind them. 'We didn't set out to play a cynical offside game,' said Martin. 'What we would do was come out of defence and push up quickly, but only on a good clearance – that was our game, otherwise we picked up opponents and got ready to defend the next attack.' It was a popular tactic during a time when the laws of the game were less circumspect to individual interpretation – if you were in an offside position then you were more often than not ruled offside. Channon was quickly able to guess Buchan's view on the goal. 'I bet he said it's still offside, didn't he?' laughed Mick. Would he have used McCalliog's pass to shoot without first bringing the ball under control? 'I probably wouldn't have, no,' said Mick, reflecting on his pace. 'But Bobby had the yard on them, you know, and he hit it early, which probably caught the keeper out – 'cos he never had an angle.'

But Mick was very quick. He would have been able to take a touch on the pass to distance himself from the chasing pack of defenders. This would have tempted Stepney out from his goal line in order to close down any angle the attacker would hope to create by moving forward with the ball. Mick would then be in a position to move the ball on to his right foot, giving him the freedom to strike it either side of Stepney, or take it around him and roll it into an unguarded net. Few players were as quick though. It's likely Bobby would have been tackled had he taken a second touch. Some match reports say Bobby ran past Martin Buchan for the goal, but the replay shows the United skipper clearly looking along the defensive line. 'Jim McCalliog played a clever first-time ball just over Brian Greenhoff's head into the gap between him and our full-back Alex Forsyth,' said Martin. 'Bobby was just off Brian's right shoulder and already on his way. Every time I see a replay of the goal Bobby is getting further and further away from our chasing back line. Once the ball was in his path we were on the half-turn and there was no catching him – not that he gave us any chance to do so.'

Bobby was blunt about his shortcomings that season in front of goal up until that moment. 'To tell the truth I missed about 20 chances in the previous six games – some were good and should have gone in. I suppose the one I scored against Hull in our last league game before the cup final gave me the confidence at the right time,' he said. Bobby may have thought he was offside but like all good professionals he played to the referee's whistle, rather than his own doubts, 'I decided what the hell – I'll knock it in anyhow.'

Southampton's Jim Steele focuses on how well Bobby took the goal. 'Some people say it was offside,' said Jim. 'I say it was a great finish – to keep the ball low like that with his left foot, too.' Despite Jim's optimism, outside of Southampton the goal is often described as dubious, not only because of the potential offside but due to the quality of the strike. It's been suggested that Bobby's goal was lucky. A fortunate goal is where the ball hits or deflects off somebody before crossing the line, or loops in directly from a cross from the wing. The powerful strike that Stepney anticipated was a reasonable prediction. Although that kind of strike tends to be more central, perhaps at waist height.

Bobby had favoured direction over pace but this gave him control over his shot. Shooting across, rather than at the keeper will always pay dividends. In England there's always been a bit of a fetish about powerfully struck shots on goal, or what's described as well hit, even if that means striking the ball down the middle of the goal where logically the goalkeeper has more chance of saving the ball. Sometimes it's as though a well-struck volley against the crossbar excites people more than a scuffed shot into the corner of the net. Had Bobby's goal been a volley, the ball hit while in the air, people would be falling over themselves.

The reality is that given ten attempts many such volleys would sail harmlessly off target, but when they do find the net that's spectacular, like a blast of a cannon. The objective remains the same though, to ensure the ball crosses the line.

Taking the strike outside the penalty area with your first touch from a ball that is coming over your shoulder is anything but fortunate. It is certainly unorthodox, particularly when taking the ball first time involves using your weaker foot. Hugh Fisher is another who says he would have taken the pass on as his left foot was his swinger. Doing so would allow you to move the ball on to your right foot if necessary, the foot you can trust to place the ball, or if necessary give it a smash. Not only was Bobby's goal not a fluke, it was also a difficult technique to execute. Next time you're playing, whether it be at the park or in a five-a-side, try it. If your team's playmaker sees you making a run and plays the ball over your shoulder, try striking the ball first time with your less favoured foot. It can end up looking foolish, clumsy even. Striking the ball cleanly in the chosen direction is not sufficient. Positionally, it requires the player to be intelligent enough to have the awareness to run into a position whereby he shapes his body such that he has the ball in front of him and is able to strike straight away.

Bobby had a quick glance as the ball bounced in front of him. If there is anything awkward about his movement it's when he's getting his body in to the right position, in what commentators like to describe as sorting out his feet. Once he'd done that he demonstrated textbook poise — using his right leg as a pivot before striking the ball.

Southampton centre-half Mel Blyth was always confident that his side could pick up the victory. 'I fancied it,' he said. 'We had nothing to lose and on the day we were the better team. I remember some of their lads coming up to me and Steeley after the game, saying, "You two had us in your pocket today." "Just one of them days," I told them. Once we scored I remember thinking, "That's it."'

Jim Steele remembers the moment he knew they'd done it. 'We had a free kick on the edge of our box and I just wanted to use up the time, so I got our left-back David Peach in close to me, but then Clive Thomas walked right up to me, picked up the ball, shook my hand and said, "Congratulations, you've won the FA Cup." I mean, what a feeling.' Blyth was pleased for Stokes, 'I was over the moon that Bobby got the goal. The little guy has taken a lot of stick recently for missing chances.'

Buchan gives Lawrie McMenemy much credit for the Saints' victory. 'His strength lay in man management; he assembled a group of mostly mature, seasoned professionals and knew how to get the best out of them. In my opinion, I think too many of our team got carried away with the pre-match hype – they thought we were going to be millionaires from our players' pool and weren't focused enough on the job in hand. If you believed the razzmatazz then we just had to turn up at Wembley to collect our medals. And we did, but they were losers' ones.'

Lenny Benham was part of the family group from Paulsgrove at Wembley to support Bobby. 'We were in tears, Bobby's goal hurt,' said Lenny. Not because of the rivalry between Portsmouth and Southampton, but because they hadn't backed Bobby as the first goalscorer and the odds of him doing so were something like 33-1. Another Paulsgrove resident, Bob Floyd, was also crying, although his emotions were on a slightly different level as he had bet on Bobby, as he said, 'Well, you've got to back the local boy, haven't you?'

13

Spotlight

THE name Brian Marchant doesn't mean a thing to people in Southampton; it should do. Once the 1976 FA Cup Final was over and the fans had left the Wembley terraces, the pundits on television were still going over the slow-motion replay of Bobby's goal, looking to prove whether or not he was onside. Meanwhile, Brian Marchant, the man who had the definitive answer, put down his red flag in the quiet of the match officials' dressing room. In terms of Southampton's history Brian's contribution is as significant as that of the Russian linesman who allowed Geoff Hurst's vital England goal against West Germany in the 1966 World Cup Final, their third of the afternoon. In reality, Tofiq Bahramov wasn't Russian, he was from Azerbaijan, but that's life for a linesman. Make a mistake and it's the hangman's rope, do something memorable and nobody tends to pick up on the exact details.

Ted Crocker was on edge. As the Football Association's secretary he didn't want English football's 1976 showpiece game overshadowed by controversy – not on his watch.

Having carried out his own post-mortem by watching the instant replay of Bobby's goal he made a beeline for the officials' room, congratulating Brian for making the right call. Ted had needed to watch the replay five times first though. Brian appreciated the sentiment, but he didn't need reassurance. He had the best view in the house and said the goal was definitely onside.

The 1976 FA Cup Final wasn't only the pinnacle of Bobby's career, it was Brian's too. He was a Herefordshire-based referee who worked as a linesman for the Football League. The referee that day was Clive Thomas, a Welshman with an idiosyncratic way of doing things, once disallowing a Brazilian goal in a World Cup match because it came as he blew his final whistle. He admitted to not being in the best position to decide whether or not Bobby was onside, although from where he stood towards the halfway line Bobby looked offside. Clive put his faith in Brian. Like Ted Crocker, he told Brian that it looked like a tough one to call. Brian disagreed, saying there was no debate.

Brian passed away a few years ago. His son Neil has kept many press cuttings from his father's career, revealing his thoughts about Bobby's goal. Nerves still played a part in officiating on the big stage, as Brian once said, 'It's not so much the 100,000 crowd that puts the fear of God into you as you wait in the players' tunnel – it's the knowledge that 40 million people will be watching the match on television.' While the FA Cup Final drew a large televised audience, the majority of them were expecting a Manchester United victory. 'If my dad had put up his flag that day there probably wouldn't have been many complaints,' said Neil. 'United were the team expected to win and TV replays weren't what they are today.' Thankfully for Southampton, Brian's judgement wasn't swayed by tricks of the mind. He held the line and kept his flag down. You can see him in the background of pretty much all the photographs of

Bobby's goal, but when the conversation turns to that goal his name is never mentioned, his views on it were never sought after. He officiated at a time when referees and linesmen were largely anonymous figures to those who went to watch the game.

The technology which provided the slow-motion replay being pored over by the TV pundits had only existed for around a decade. Writing on the subject for the FA's yearbook in 1976, Jimmy Hill relayed the fears of referees and linesmen when he wondered if this new technology might hang them out to dry. Although much maligned as a pundit himself, Jimmy's fears have been proved right. The technology was developed by now-defunct US electronics company Ampex. The HS-100 video disc recorder, as it was known, looked more like a souped-up record deck than groundbreaking technology. At £70,000 it wasn't cheap either. To put the expense into context the record British transfer fee for a player at that time was still the £350,000 Everton paid Birmingham City for Bob Latchford. It needn't have mattered to Brian. The television people could go on and on about Bobby's goal, but they didn't have the most important angle, the one he had along the last line of United's defence.

But Brian's afternoon wasn't over after that. As he gathered his belongings he noticed he had been presented with the wrong medal – a runners-up one, as opposed to the medals given to the match officials. He had to go to United's dressing room to swap it. The medal turned out to be Martin Buchan's, the very man who led the protests about the legitimacy of Bobby's goal. Brian's arrival in the United dressing room was met by what he described as good-natured banter. He would have needed some resolve to set foot in there though. It was a different time. It's difficult to imagine such a restrained greeting for a linesman in those circumstances during Alex Ferguson's tenure at Old Trafford, when he would react to what he believed to be a dubious goal – that is, one scored against his team – with the frantic injustice of someone who's had the gusset of their underpants daubed with Deep Heat. But the goal wasn't dubious to Brian – it was perfectly legitimate. By day he was a fruit buyer for cider maker Bulmers, and within a week of the cup final he was refereeing a cup match at a local police ground in Herefordshire, which as he said, 'was all in the game'. His teenage grandsons now referee; what chance of them one day doing so at St Mary's? If they did so it's highly unlikely many would know the significance.

On the day, Southampton fans were far too preoccupied with the sense of achievement, so carrying out a post-mortem on the legitimacy of Bobby's goal was not high on the agenda. They headed back south after the game while the players stayed in London. 'Oh, it was unbelievable,' said Hugh Fisher. 'We made a mistake though, we should have come back to Southampton after the game, but we stayed in London that night. Don't get me wrong, we were hooting and hollering; we went to a club called the Talk of the Town. We'd had a bit to drink, so we probably upset a few people's evenings who were looking over their shoulders and thinking, who the hell are this rabble. The BBC were there too, it was chaos.' Southampton city centre would have been a very obliging host to the players – the pubs were packed on the Saturday night, with many staying open well into the early hours.

Bobby joined his team-mates on the Sunday for an open-top bus tour of Southampton. The skies were overcast and grey. The long, hot summer of 1976 had yet to take hold of the country, and the communal grass of parks and verges was still a few months shy of resembling the straw-baked yellow of a cricket wicket. The tour of the city was planned to take an hour. More than 200,000 people turned up so it ended up taking three. Southampton supporters of all intensities came out in their numbers to see the team parade the trophy. They were self-aware enough to realise this could well be a one-off opportunity.

The sheer weight of traffic entering the city threatened to prevent some of the players reaching the bus. Mel Blyth drove down to Southampton from Surrey, getting stuck in a queue at the top of the avenue which leads into the city. The roads were packed with fans and Mel was growing ever more impatient, a flurry of coarse language directed at the stationary obstacles ahead of him.

He started sounding his horn. 'I was getting the hump,' said Mel. 'Then two cars down this big geezer – massive, he was – gets out and starts walking towards me.' There was anger written all over his face, so Mel knew he had a problem, 'He was about to have a right go at me, then he went, Mel Blyth? He started shouting, fucking hell, it's Mel Blyth. Everybody, get out of the way, it's Mel Blyth.' Mel went from getting a knuckle sandwich to having the road cleared and a police escort to the open-top bus – it was the kind of rare occasion when road rage gave way to generosity of spirit.

The city tour was an opportunity for Bobby to try and make sense of it all. Less than 24 hours had passed since he had scored Southampton's most famous goal. It was a lot to take on board. He'd gone into the previous day's cup final on the transfer list and out of scoring form, but he left Wembley stadium as the man responsible for the club's first major trophy. He could be heard repeating himself; telling those around him that he couldn't shoot with his left foot, and that he thought he was offside anyway, but just hit it and hoped. He was reflective, too, saying that he'd agreed to come off the transfer list after eight months; that he'd been fed up, but that he couldn't be fed up anymore, could he?

Like much of the city, Bobby was in a daze. He had woken up in a new world, but it wasn't him who had changed, it was the world around him. The logic he had used seven years earlier to deal with the nerves and expectation of his Southampton debut as a teenager could not be applied to this situation. The stakes were that much higher this time around. Two days beforehand he was looking over his shoulder, wondering where his career would take him. The only thing in the rear-view mirror now was pats on the back. It wasn't a case of not being able to handle the attention; it was more to do with not being able to fully understand it. Grasping what he'd achieved against the backdrop of this new-found adulation was a totally alien experience for him, one perhaps he never fully understood or came to terms with.

But it went deeper than that. It wasn't only a lack of understanding, his goal brought with it a weight of responsibility, one that Lawrie McMenemy questions whether Bobby would have chosen to carry if he'd had any choice in the matter. 'Bobby was a lovely lad, but if you're going to win 1-0 in a historic moment Bobby probably wouldn't have wanted to have been the one that scored the goal because the spotlight moved on to him in a big way,' said Lawrie. 'He didn't like it really, not underneath. If somebody like Mick Channon or Peter Osgood had scored the winner, or even Jim McCalliog, or Peter Rodrigues, coming up taking a penalty, then people wouldn't have been all that surprised. Those players would have been able to take it in their stride. Everybody had heard of them – they were English, Scottish and Welsh internationals who had all played at Wembley before. They were used to the attention and the media interviews that went with that. This wasn't the case with Bobby. It was a fresh story for the newspapers. All of a sudden, against all the odds, Southampton win the FA Cup, and who's this fella who scored the goal? Let's find out,' said Lawrie, explaining how the media approached the story.

'It was a great angle for the newspapers – they were uncovering a new name, but Bobby didn't want that, he didn't bask or revel in it – he shied away. From then on, wherever Bobby went he was known. Don't get me wrong, he loved to score goals and I wasn't surprised he scored it, but I don't think he welcomed the attention that came with it.'

The attention Lawrie spoke of began as soon as referee Clive Thomas blew the final whistle. ITV presenter Brian Moore handed over from the studio to Gerald Sinstadt, who was somewhere in the bowels of Wembley Stadium. With his khaki safari jacket, orange buttoned-down shirt and horn-rimmed spectacles, Sinstadt looked as though he'd walked straight in from the Open University. Bobby stood beside him, a half-drunk glass bottle of milk in one hand, the FA Cup in the other. Several of his team-mates stood behind him. Peter Osgood towered above Bobby, beaming like a proud parent, as Sinstadt introduced Bobby as the man responsible for winning Southampton the cup. Bobby sighed, not only as though to dismiss the pomp and ceremony he was being associated with, but as though he could scarcely believe it himself.

Bobby agreed with Sinstadt that it was the happiest day of his life before he was asked to explain how he nearly left the club before Christmas, 'Yeah, down the road to my local Pompey, but the move wasn't right so I stayed with the boys.' Peter Osgood led the cheers of delight in the background. Sinstadt then asked Bobby to run over his thoughts on the goal over a televised reply, 'It just bounced up right for me,' said Bobby, as he cast his eye on the replay on a small television screen in the foreground. Aware that his colleagues were pleased, he played up to the gallery before once again being quick to deflect praise

Anyone for tennis? Bobby (centre in the front row) with the Paulsgrove Secondary Modern tennis team. Courtesy of Mark Newman

Rising star – Bobby (third from right in bottom row) as part of the Paulsgrove Secondary Modern football team.

International bright young thing – Bobby (fourth from the left in bottom row) with the England youth team in 1969. Courtesy of Keith Eccleshare

Southampton go mad – Bobby's strike beats Alex Stepney and wins Southampton the 1976 FA Cup. Courtesy of the Daily Echo

Onside – Brian Marchant (left) the linesman who ruled Bobby's goal onside at Wembley, with Alf Gray. Photo courtesy of Neil Marchant

Bobby with the FA Cup and Peter Osgood in the bath at Wembley. Courtesy of the Daily Echo

Bobby gets used to the attention of scoring a cup final winning goal.
Courtesy of the Daily Echo

Bobby with his dad in the garden in Paulsgrove in 1976.

A Saints shirt in Portsmouth. Left to right: Bobby's cousin Maria Johnson, in the Southampton shirt he wore in the FA Cup semi-final, Bobby Stokes, his mum Marjorie, and Aunt Helen. Courtesy of Maria Johnson

Street party: Leominster Road in Paulsgrove gets ready to welcome Bobby home from Wembley. Courtesy of Maria Johnson

’Ello ’ello – Bobby poses with local police in Paulsgrove with the Golden Boot he was presented for scoring Southampton’s winning goal in the FA Cup Final. Photo courtesy of Maria Johnson

Bobby and his Uncle Albie back in Paulsgrove the day after Southampton won the 1976 FA Cup.

Bobby at the Dell with the Ford Granada he won for scoring the winning goal in the 1976 FA Cup Final.

Bobby at work
at the Harbour
View Cafe in
Portsmouth in
the early 1990s.

Back at
Wembley:
Bobby was
there to cheer
Southampton
on in the 1992
Zenith Data
Systems Cup
Final.

elsewhere, 'It was in the moment it left my foot, you know,' said Bobby. 'But people like Jim McCalliog, Peter Osgood, Mick Channon and Peter Rodrigues did a great job in helping the team get settled into the game.'

It was left for Channon to blow Bobby's trumpet, with his own unique way of summing up the goal, 'Christ, the lad didn't half hit it well – he's the best at the club at it – we've been saying it for so long.' Along with his medal Bobby was presented with a golden boot, which today is more commonly associated with the prize given to the top goalscorer in either the World Cup finals or the top divisions throughout Europe.

The Football Association ran the initiative during the 1970s, presenting the scorer of the winning goal in the FA Cup Final with the prize. The boot was produced by Coventry-based plating technology company Precious Metal Depositors, who went through the complicated process of using a real football boot to lay on layers of metal before a final coat of gold.

Bobby was presented with it at Southampton Guildhall by city mayor Elinor Pugh. It was only just starting to sink in for Bobby and his instinct was to talk about home, 'Now it's a great feeling sitting back looking at a winner's medal,' he said. 'The only one I've ever seen before was the one Jimmy Gabriel won at Everton. Now I'll be able to take this one round to show the lads at the Beehive at Portsmouth – my local.' Bobby was true to his word. 'You couldn't move in Paulsgrove,' said Maria, who still wore Bobby's red and white Southampton shirt from the semi-final during the celebrations. 'That was the best night the Beehive ever had, wasn't it dad?' Albie nodded. 'We did all the pubs that night – the Beehive, the Plover, the Beacon.' Bobby was recognised as a local hero and on that day in 1976 Paulsgrove became a shrine to Southampton's finest hour.

The celebrations went into a third day, with Mick Channon's testimonial played on the Monday night. He couldn't have planned it better, although it was a gamble. Had they lost the cup final there's no doubt there wouldn't have been anything like the scenes at The Dell that night, when a crowd of 29,508 paid their £1 entry to squeeze on to the terraces. Bobby was presented with his other prize for scoring the winner, a Ford Granada worth something in the region of £4,000.

He was photographed prior to the testimonial sat on the car bonnet and waving at the crowd, his feet dangling some way short of the grass beneath. Queens Park Rangers were the opponents that night, playing their part in an entertaining 2-2 draw. Bobby was on a roll, scoring the two Southampton goals and nearly setting up a winner which was denied only by inadvertent defending by Southampton fans from the Milton Road end who had spilled on to the pitch. It didn't matter. The testimonial was merely the stage for further celebration. When the parties stopped the spotlight remained on Bobby and it wasn't limited to being sought out by the media, it also came in the form of local grass roots football.

Don Divers founded Hedge End Rangers, a children's football club situated off junction eight of the M27, back in the early 1970s, when local youth leagues didn't exist in the size and variety they do today. Although now approaching his 80s, Don is still very much involved with the club and says, 'I'm there most Sundays, watching games.' Memories of the history of the club occupy several large envelopes, all bulging with various newspaper cuttings, football programmes and other memorabilia all accrued over the course of more than 40 seasons. A photograph spills out on to the floor of a team of boys in sky blue Hedge End Rangers jerseys, which Don instantly recognises, 'That was our first team kit – I think I paid 15 quid for the whole set from the sports shop in Woolston – they're not that cheap now.'

Don managed to pull off a huge coup in getting Bobby associated with the club shortly after Southampton's FA Cup win. 'He was involved very heavily with us during the early days. It all started when my son did a building job for Bobby's dad in Paulsgrove,' said Don. His son passed on his contact details to Don, who was not one to leave a stone unturned, making a speculative drive down to Paulsgrove on the off chance he could ask David Stokes if Bobby would be interested in being involved with Hedge End. David agreed to pass the message on to Bobby, who agreed.

The cup final was still very fresh in people's minds when Bobby handed out the awards at the club's end-of-season presentation in June 1977. 'He used to just come to training and games,' said Don. 'But I don't always know how he got there.' Hedge End was a good ten to 15 miles from Bobby's house in Southsea. With no direct train line he'd be reliant on lifts. It didn't stop Bobby turning up on a regular basis to the club's training sessions, volunteering his services as referee in a match between the boys and their parents, before accepting Don's offer of becoming honorary club president. The buzz this created helped gather the momentum for Don to get the club its own ground, which in turn provided the opportunity for many local boys to play grass roots football.

Some of Bobby's former playing colleagues look back and say he was unable to say no to the constant requests to open schools and fetes, and various engagements involving grass roots football. However, having not even met Don, let alone spoken to him, he could have quite easily never returned the call. But Bobby's sense of duty weighed upon him to the extent that he felt obliged to help, knowing that not doing so would be a disappointment to Don. But Don felt Bobby enjoyed doing things for children he didn't have himself. In Bobby's absence the cup final win maintains a presence in the area. Very rarely will a day pass when Lawrie McMenemy is not asked about it. 'At least one person will stop me in town and tell me where they were in 1976,' said Lawrie, who recalled meeting Roberto Martinez a few years back at a league managers' dinner, 'We'd never met, but he seemed down. I asked him what was up, as he'd just won the FA Cup with Wigan.' Martinez was downbeat because his side had just been relegated from the Premier League. 'I said in 30 or 40 years, people in Wigan will remember winning the cup,' said Lawrie. 'That's exactly what's happened in Southampton.'

History was relentless – it was always there, whispering incessantly in the background. Lenny Benham checked in to see Bobby a few days after the cup final. 'He was just sat there,' said Lenny. 'He told me he didn't ever want to score a winner in a cup final ever again, because everyone wanted a piece of him – the phone never stopped ringing.' For the vast majority, the pinnacle of English football is something only experienced vicariously as a spectator. On the surface Bobby's comments could have been thrown back at him by those who would have done almost anything to be in his shoes. But the perceptions of reality were off kilter. Bobby didn't pursue attention. Chunks of his life now revolved around sharpening the self-deprecating skills he used to dummy a compliment into the path of others. It later developed into a point blank refusal to accept any pats on the back for his part in history without adding in his own caveat that it was all about the team around him, or that he was offside.

14

The Break-Up

J IM Steele leant on a table and sighed, 'Yeah, I messed up – the ball ran under my foot and Van Der Elst scored, but we should have been five bloody nil up by then.' He was talking about his mistake that led to Anderlecht knocking Southampton out of the quarter-finals of the 1976/77 European Cup Winners' Cup. The Belgian side were the competition's defending champions, taking a 2-0 first-leg lead to The Dell. Southampton gave them a scare, going two up with 13 minutes still left to play in the return leg, but Van Der Elst's goal killed the game. As a last roll of the dice, Bobby was brought on as a substitute for defender Manny Andruszewski with five minutes left. It was his final appearance in the Southampton first team.

In May 1977, around six weeks after the exit from Europe, Bobby was signed by Washington Diplomats of the North American Soccer League (NASL) for what was reported to have been a small fee. It was just under a year after the FA Cup Final. There was no great fanfare, there wasn't even a whole page dedicated to the news in the local paper – Bobby had to share his goodbye, fighting for space on the page with the latest county cricket scores and an announcement by the Ministry of Agriculture, who were planning on resuming the gassing of badgers in Gloucestershire. In some ways the world of football was even more cut-throat in 1977 than it is today. Bobby had been unable to kick on after the cup final, finding himself a peripheral figure on the fringes of Southampton's starting line-up in the season that followed. The world of 24-hour rolling sports news was some way off, so the media's role was simply to report on the transfer, rather than wallow in any nostalgia. Time had simply moved on at The Dell and Bobby hadn't been able to keep pace with it.

The build-up to Bobby's and Jim's last season at The Dell was promising. It suggested a different future than the one that was soon to materialise. Southampton's pre-season form ahead of 1976/77 included winning the Tennent Caledonian Cup, when they beat Rangers 2-1 in the final at Ibrox. Good fortune seemed to be on their side. Their semi-final with Manchester City went to a penalty shoot-out in which all 22 players had scored their kicks. Rather than continue taking penalties until somebody missed, the result was decided on the toss of a coin, which Southampton won.

Manchester City's Dennis Tueart, an FA Cup winner with Sunderland in 1973, took the opportunity to talk to Lawrie McMenemy during the shoot-out preparations. He hoped Southampton didn't make the same mistakes as his former club in using their forward momentum by getting promoted to the First Division at the first time of asking. Lawrie was crystal clear on where he stood with anyone thinking the cup final meant they had made it, 'I know the problems and I've got to stop people floating away in the clouds. If anybody wants to strut around with the cup winner's medal round his neck he'll find it's just another way of strangling himself.'

Then it was back to Wembley, this time the Charity Shield against defending league champions Liverpool. Southampton lost 1-0. Paul Gilchrist may have vivid memories of the cup final but the Charity Shield remains a complete blur. 'I couldn't tell you anything about the game other than how hot it was that day – it was such a draining experience,' said Paul. Bobby toiled for the 90 minutes, but Liverpool were in complete control. There was no shame in losing to the defending league champions but Mick Channon saw things differently. He went in thinking Southampton could win. He felt that as a group they could give anyone a game. They would get no further chance to prove that. It was the last time that the starting line-up from the FA Cup Final would play together. Hugh Fisher became player-manager at Southport, Jim McCalliog was signed by Chicago Sting before a spell at Lincoln City as player-coach, while Peter Rodrigues called it a day after being unable to shrug off a nagging knee injury.

Paul says Lawrie was determined not to follow in Sunderland's footsteps. 'He called us in for a chat during pre-season and warned us we all had half a dozen games to prove ourselves,' said Paul. 'Then we lost the first game of the season at home to Carlisle.' This game saw Southampton get off to the worst possible start, going a goal down after 30 seconds. Southampton equalised, but Carlisle won 2-1. Paul and Bobby were dropped for the next match as the Saints endured an indifferent run of form. This included 4-0 and 6-2 losses to Hull City and Charlton Athletic respectively. They had to wait until October for first their league win, by which time Bobby had lost his starting place.

By now Paul had played his last game for the club. Having played in the cup final and then the Charity Shield he appeared just three more times. A move to Saudi Arabia proved to be a disaster: the football was of a far poorer standard than he had been advised and he made a quick return to the UK, signing for Ian St John's Third Division Portsmouth in March 1977. It highlighted how precarious a football career could be. Paul's spectacular goals in the fifth round replay against West Brom and the semi-final against Crystal Palace deserved to leave an indelible mark on the club's history.

When Bobby left the club, Lawrie McMenemy told reporters that he had been a good servant for Southampton and would always be remembered for the goal he scored in the cup final. It was true enough. But that alone was insufficient to maintain a place in the team. Today, Lawrie confesses to not remembering exactly why Bobby was forced out of the side. 'You'd have to look it up,' he said, before asking if perhaps Bobby had been injured. The main reason for Bobby's move was the arrival of Ted MacDougall, who joined in September from Norwich City. Unlike Bobby, MacDougall was an out-and-out striker, who scored 26 goals during his first season with Southampton. The mention of MacDougall jogs Lawrie's memory, 'Ah well, if Ted MacDougall was there, Phil Bowyer would have been there as well.' Like MacDougall, Bowyer was a prolific scorer for Southampton. He did sign in 1977, but not until Bobby had already left. With regular striker Mick Channon one goal short of MacDougall's 26 and Peter Osgood continuing to be used as a target man, there was little room for Bobby.

When players were out of the team they'd want to talk to the manager. 'If any player wasn't getting a regular game then as manager you'd get a knock on the door,' said Lawrie. 'I'd then have to make a decision – if they're on a contract then they need to work harder, force their way in. As manager you don't have to be liked, but you have to be respected. MacDougall scored a lot of goals, and had a good partnership with Bowyer; then when he left people were concerned – but Bowyer went on to be top scorer on his own. Things move on, and decisions aren't always popular, but a big part of management is about making decisions. Scoring the winner at Wembley doesn't guarantee you a regular game; it guarantees you fame and a place in history and nobody should deny that.'

Being dropped was the same for all players under Lawrie's tenure. 'You'd always take them to one side,' said Lawrie. 'Every player wants to know why they're out of the team, so you tell them. If they don't agree then you tell them that that is the decision. If the decision doesn't work out then sometimes the manager has to hold his hands up.' While Lawrie tried to be consistent in how he did things, it sometimes proved difficult when players were reaching the crossroads of their careers. 'It can be a little more tricky with older players. Alan Ball was coming to the end of his career when we bought him, but he wanted to play every game.' Then there was big centre-half John McGrath. Lawrie was the one who had to call him in to say it's time to pack in. 'He knew it was time,' said Lawrie. 'Players don't want to admit it, but deep down they know.' Lawrie had the necessary strength of character to break the bad news. 'Making decisions is the biggest part of the job,' he added.

Bob McCarthy was released by Southampton in 1975. He'd had a cartilage operation at 17 but the problem flared up again later in his career. 'It's a cut-throat business,' said Bob. 'There were 12 players there in the first team squad on a Saturday afternoon, but loads of others are hidden away in the background. My contract was up at the end of the 1974/75 season. I was called into the manager's office and told I wasn't needed anymore, thank you very much.' Paul Bennett was in the same boat at the end of the following season. It was made clear he didn't have a future at the club and that was that. There were no agents, as a player you were on your own.

There was still time for Bobby to have some new experiences during that final season at The Dell. He played in the 4-0 win over Marseille in the first round of the European Cup Winners' Cup. There was also a trip to Italy, as part of the short-lived Anglo-Italian League Cup, which saw Italy's Coppa Italia winners play the victors of the FA Cup in a fairly needless two-legged final. Hugh Fisher remembers it well. With Peter Rodrigues injured, he was made captain but Southampton's 1-0 win at The Dell wasn't sufficient to win the trophy. 'We got absolutely murdered over there,' said Hugh, reflecting on the 4-0 loss. 'But it was a bit of a jolly.' Hugh and Bobby were strolling around the city on the afternoon of the game looking for a bite to eat. 'We found a little pizza place,' said Hugh. 'There was a guy there with a young lad in a wheelchair. Being the lad he was Bobby felt sorry for the boy, going over to him to say hello and putting an arm around his shoulder.' The boy misinterpreted Bobby's good intentions, delivering a fairly robust punch into Bobby. 'A big crowd gathered round,' said Hugh. 'All these Italian guys were apologising; of course back at the hotel the lads thought it was hilarious.'

Foreign trips aside, Bobby spent much of his game time back with the reserves. Kevin Dawtry was a teenager at The Dell at the time and this was the perfect opportunity for Bobby to start throwing his weight around. But although he was naturally disappointed to be out of the team he did not become the big-time Charlie that the occasion suggested he could. So Kevin's formative years in Southampton's second team were not exposed to any fits of rage. 'Bobby was always cheerful,' remembered Kevin. 'He always had a quiet word of advice.'

Games were usually played at stadiums, so it would mean playing at Highbury, or White Hart Lane, as well as The Dell, but as Roger Fry said, once you'd had a taste of the first team, reserve football wasn't quite the same.

The fifth round draw for the 1977 FA Cup gave Manchester United the opportunity to avenge the previous year's defeat in the final. Southampton lost the replay 2-1 at Old Trafford having drawn 2-2 at The Dell. Bobby was conspicuous by his absence from the two games. By the time they saw out the season in ninth place in the Second Division, Bobby had already gone. The move marked the end of 11 years at The Dell – nine of which were as a full-time professional. Bobby scored 55 Southampton goals in 238 appearances, finishing as the club's second-highest goalscorer with 13 in 1973/74 and 1975/76. The statistics alone don't reflect the role he played, linking midfield with attack. These were the days before heat maps and all wealth of statistics that could prove and demonstrate the work he put into his game. His team-mates didn't need that evidence, they saw and felt his contribution on a regular basis.

Bobby had turned the move to the US down at first. He'd already arranged to get married in June and was wary that signing for a club who played a season that ran from April to August might jeopardise his wedding plans. His new employers made special dispensation for Bobby to fly back to the UK to get married in Portsmouth, although the newlyweds' honeymoon had to wait until the end of the NASL season.

The Anderlecht game was not his last in the red and white stripes though; that came on a Monday night at The Dell in a reserve fixture with Plymouth Argyle. The writing was on the wall for Bobby. He did his usual thing, working the space between midfield and attack. There were 402 there to see them lose 4-2. It's doubtful they knew this was Bobby's curtain call.

He could at least look forward to some company in the States. Goalkeeper Eric Martin had joined Washington two years earlier. Jim Steele made the same move in April, playing just one further game for Southampton after the Anderlecht tie before being transferred. He was very sorry to be leaving. Many Southampton fans felt the same. Jim remains a popular figure among those who remember his man-of-the-match performance at the centre of Southampton's defence in the 1976 FA Cup Final, where he followed ferocious challenges with nonchalant passes with the outside of his boot. Mention his name to those supporters and they might even break into song, 'Six-foot two, eyes are blue – Jimmy Steele is after you.' Although 40 years have passed many are still keen to chat with him about his playing days.

Jim remains an imposing figure. Not only tall, but broad-shouldered. When he pats you on the back you get the impression he could still clobber a centre-forward or two. 'The knees aren't so good, but I don't feel my age – I can still run,' said Jim. The idea of being the age of a pensioner doesn't sit well with him. Tell him that 65 is not really that old these days and he disagrees. 'It's fucking ancient,' said Jim, who rated Bobby. 'As a player, he was a bit like Alan Ball – full of energy.'

The years spent living outside Scotland are only occasionally revealed in the flattened vowels that can be heard when he says 'mate'. Jim sometimes drinks at the Two Brothers, a pub on the western suburban outskirts of Southampton. He remains fond of the club. When his mobile rings it lights up revealing a screen saver photograph of the FA Cup winning team with the trophy at Wembley.

I met Jim at the Two Brothers one weekday afternoon, where he quickly introduced me to a few others at the bar. 'The lad's writing a book about Stokesy,' he said. Before I had the chance to say a word a pint of lager appeared on the bar in front of me. The man who bought it then introduced himself as Jag, before pulling out his tablet computer from his coat pocket and asking me if I'd seen *this*. I nodded; it was a YouTube video of Bobby's winning Wembley goal. 'Bobby Stokes is a legend of the club, do you know?' he said, before prodding me on the arm to make sure I was listening. I blabbered something about there no longer being anything at St Mary's to commemorate him. Jag's smile vanished, and was quickly replaced with something closely resembling disgust. He looked surprised, almost angry, 'Nothing? We need to make this happen – now.' He banged his clenched fist on the bar. In the 30 seconds I'd known Jag he'd bought me a drink, showed me a video and somehow made me feel personally responsible for the lack of anything Bobby-related in the city. He fumbled in his pockets for his mobile phone. 'We need a statue of him at St Mary's. We can make it happen – I know people, people with money. I'll make a donation – what's your number?' We exchanged telephone numbers, before he got distracted by another conversation near the fruit machine.

I offered to give Jim a lift home. There were two cars parked outside – a Mercedes and my dilapidated Peugeot 306 estate. Jim seemed to be heading for the former, causing me to point in the direction of my Peugeot, which he tried to open, sensing my key had a wireless unlocking mechanism. Jim adjusted the seat to accommodate his height as he explained he was not directly involved with the Ex-Saints Association anymore. 'Perhaps they're worried about my reputation,' said Jim, who makes no secret of his enjoyment of a few lunchtime pints. It seems like a fair trade-off for the man of the match in the 1976 FA Cup Final. To put it bluntly, Jim was never going to be someone who spent his retirement trying to solve Sudoku puzzles or playing carpet bowls. Jim's final epitaph for Bobby was short and to the point, 'He was as straight as a die, not like some bastards.'

15

Take That, Pelé

BOBBY'S move to the States in 1977 coincided with the farewell tour of one of the greatest players in the history of the game. Pelé was due to leave New York Cosmos at the end of the season; he wasn't just leaving the North American Soccer League (NASL), but retiring from competitive football altogether. This was not lost on the public relations and marketing departments of every club in the league. American sports fans with no prior interest in soccer knew who Pelé was. The visit of the Cosmos to teams around the country meant it was far more likely people would pay to watch. Maybe they'd come back again if it was a good game. It might have been time up for Pelé, but not for Bobby. He was 26. There was still plenty of time to kick-start his career in the States.

Alongside Jim Steele and Eric Martin, Bobby played against some of the most recognised names in world football, the biggest of which was undoubtedly Pelé. Jim enjoys explaining the experience of man-marking the Brazilian. 'You'd show him one way and he'd just go the over,' said Jim, adopting a defensive position to demonstrate his point, hunkering down with his knees slightly bent. 'I would show him the outside and he'd play the ball off my shins to go inside – what a jammy bastard! But I suppose it's no fluke if you do it about eight times.' Mike Dillon later played alongside Bobby and Jim at the Dips, but in 1977 he was on the playing roster for the Cosmos. It wasn't only the money at their disposal and the star names they were able to attract that separated the Cosmos from the Dips, as Mike explained, 'The main difference between playing for the two sides was the crowds. People came out in big numbers to watch the Cosmos.' This was no different when the Cosmos came to Robert F. Kennedy Memorial (RFK) Stadium in Washington, with more than 30,000 fans showing up to watch.

Bobby had a good start, scoring on his debut in a 2-1 win over Chicago Sting at Soldier Field. He was rewarded with a bear hug from Jim Steele. More noticeable about the goal was the swathes of empty seats in the background. Soldier Field was home to Chicago Bears and able to host 60,000 people. The 2,000 there to see Bobby's goal were lost in the emptiness. The set-up of the league was a little back to front. They had the stadiums, but not always the fans to fill them, not unless Pelé was in town. But that only happened once a season. This lack of fans at some grounds fed into a further responsibility of the players. Part of the job was to spread word of the game. Players would do these football clinics at local schools, explaining and demonstrating how to play. Many of the stadiums would have been an eye-opener for British players.

RFK was also home to American football's Washington Redskins, who would regularly pull in home crowds of more than 50,000 during the NFL season. The majority of the stadiums in the US bore more resemblance to the stadiums we have in the UK today, than the grounds Bobby and Jim had left behind in the 1970s. RFK was an all-seater, two-tiered bowl stadium. For Diplomats games it only tended to open the lower tier. Attendances were pretty good bearing in mind the club was still in its infancy. They'd regularly have between 15,000 and 20,000 fans for home games, which was considerably higher than the meagre 1,000 or so people who showed up to watch them in Connecticut. But the owners of the franchise wanted crowds to average 20,000. The players had to do what they could to pull them in – their careers depended on it.

Bobby followed up his goal in Chicago with two more the following week in Seattle against a Sounders side featuring Harry Redknapp. Next came the new experience of a shoot-out. Unable to tolerate the idea of a game which produced no winner, the NASL decided the outcome of all tied games with a shoot-out. It wasn't decided on penalty kicks, though. Instead, players would stand with the ball 35 yards from goal. On the referee's whistle they had five seconds to score. Bobby got a taste of this in California when the Dips played San Jose. The Spartan Stadium was far more of a football ground than a stadium. In their eagerness to get a good view of the shootout, many fans left their position in the stands to watch the action on a grass bank behind the goal. Bobby took three touches in his shoot-out attempt – the third a right-footed strike from just inside the D of the penalty area that found the onrushing goalkeeper's bottom-left corner. It led the Dips to a win on the road.

Teams would play opposition from all over the country but the points they won went towards competing in mini leagues for a place in the play-offs. Competing in the Eastern Division, Washington would always play second fiddle to the most recognisable name in the franchise – New York Cosmos. Having played mostly on grass, this game was on the artificial carpet at New York's Meadowlands Stadium – home of American football's

New York Giants. This was an occupational hazard in the NASL. There seemed to be mistrust of the surface among some British players; an inability or stubborn refusal to adapt to the new conditions. Footwear was an issue. Studs were off-limits on Astroturf, although some still wore them. There are pictures of George Best playing for Los Angeles Aztecs, giving chase to Pelé while wearing moulded studs. Pounding the hard surface with studded boots was a surefire guarantee of serious and unnecessary blisters. But the surface at the Cosmos wasn't the kind many of us are familiar with at our local sports ground or school.

It had more in common with the spiky green baize used as a display on some fruit and veg market stalls. Players complained that it would bunch up beneath their feet. Flat soles were more forgiving. Eric Martin called them samba shoes. Samba as in the Adidas Samba, lightweight and other than a series of token indents on the sole, offering no grip whatsoever. Such shoes are wholly fit for purpose in a bit of five-a-side on an indoor hard court against say, Steve from accounts and some of the lads from the warehouse in a knock-about after work, but not Pelé – one of the greatest players to have ever lived.

Bobby got on the scoresheet in shoes people now tend to wear with jeans, but the Dips got pulverised with the Cosmos putting eight goals past them. It was a lousy result. Naturally, many of the Dips' playing roster were touchy on the subject. Not just about the defeat though, but also the nature of the facilities they played on. Having damaged a cartilage in his knee during a pre-season tour in New Zealand, Tottenham Hotspur's Don McAllister had been loaned out to Washington to regain full fitness. He wasn't impressed with the artificial playing surface in New York. 'We'd been playing on grass all year, so it was a waste of time playing on that,' insisted Don. 'I think they watered it before the game – the ball was sliding and bouncing all over the place.' Then there was Pelé to contend with. Pelé was 36 back in 1977, but far from past it where Don's concerned, 'We're talking about perhaps the greatest player to have ever played the game and he wasn't hampered by injuries. He was out of this world.'

The Cosmos, and Pelé in particular, highlighted how a team who were used to playing on artificial pitches were more than likely to murder anyone who wasn't. The Dips were unable to judge the bounce or pace of the ball. When a forward pass was played towards Pelé, Don anticipated it would bounce up towards his chest. Instead it kicked up in the direction of Don's face. Having failed to anticipate the run of the ball Don was temporarily out of the game and Pelé was on his bike, crashing a shot against Eric Martin's crossbar. The Dips were chasing shadows and the Cosmos revelled in it.

Eric Martin was wearing shorts. His legs got cut every time he dived, which was quite a lot, not that he was one to rant and rave, 'Once it's done, it's done.' He'd far prefer to impart advice quietly. He didn't roast players in front of the fans. 'We knew we could match them on grass at our place though,' said Don. And they did. In a strange quirk of the fixture list they hosted the Cosmos just ten days later having already played a further two fixtures. The extra games did little for confidence; they lost 3-0 to Vancouver Whitecaps and 4-1 to Connecticut. This left the Dips at the bottom of the four-team Eastern Conference. The thrashing in New York was bad enough but now some of their players were putting the boot in off the field, with Cosmos striker Steve Hunt describing the Dips as the worst team they'd played all season.

This turned things up a notch when it came to publicity. The game had been a dead rubber, but with Pelé's farewell tour and a bit of bad blood it had something riding on it.

Jim Steele fought fire with fire, telling the *Washington Post* that they'd 'take care' of Hunt in the rematch. You didn't need a dictionary to work out what he had planned. But before they ripped into the enemy there was plenty of time for Jim and Bobby to socialise with them first. Jim and Bobby normally spent the Friday before a Sunday game playing golf. On this occasion he was summoned by the manager to go to a press conference and take one of the guys with him. 'I'm thinking, press conference, what press conference? So I get Bobby to come with me,' said Jim. 'It was at a hotel and the car park was packed. The hotel lobby was packed as well, but once we'd made our way through the crowds we sat at a table ready to be questioned, then someone came over and asked us if we wanted a drink, so naturally we said yes. They brought some Budweiser over. Then they get to Pelé and he said no – he doesn't drink in the lead-up to a game. I'm thinking, Christ, he's made us look bad already, and on TV too.'

Such press conferences were regularly televised. The focus here was on Pelé and if he would win the Soccer Bowl in his last season. Pelé talked and sipped water. Jim said, 'Pelé was very much aware of his public image. Later on he told us he liked to relax just like anyone else, but because he was a role model to so many children around the world he chose to lay off the drink, in front of the cameras, anyway. After the press conference, Pelé's people asked me and Bobby if we wanted to come up to his hotel suite.' It was full with all the various hangers-on and PR men and wives and girlfriends. 'Pelé sees me and says, "You Scottish?"' said Jim. 'Aye, I nodded. Then he tells me he loves Scotch whisky and cracked open a bottle.' Good times were had. For all we know Bobby and Pelé could well have seen the evening out doing karaoke to Elton John and Kiki Dee, but the ensuing almost 40 years has eroded the memory to its barest essence.

They had a day to recover. The programme notes had Bobby as doubtful of playing because of a strained hamstring, but he showed resilience and shook this off. As far as Eric was concerned one thing was certain about the forthcoming Cosmos game, 'You have good games and you have bad ones. The only thing I knew for sure was that the Cosmos would not score eight goals again.' It was an accurate prediction. It was the last game of the regular season and the Cosmos had already qualified for the play-offs, clinching second spot in the Eastern Conference. This meant home advantage in the first round of the play-offs. They weren't prepared to lighten up against the Dips though. Beckenbauer and Chinaglia were rested, but Pelé played. So did Werner Roth, who is perhaps best known for having his penalty saved by the Allies' goalkeeper Hatch, played by Sylvester Stallone, in the 1981 film *Escape to Victory*. The Cosmos game attracted 31,000 fans into RFK.

Jim Redfern put the Dips two goals up in the opening half an hour. Pelé pulled one back from the penalty spot before half-time, but the bigger talking point was the number of players taking to the field in the second half. Having had two sent off the Dips had to play the entire second period with nine men. The playing field was levelled slightly when the Cosmos were reduced to ten, but the lack of numbers shaped the Dips' tactics. By this time Bobby's socks were rolled down by his ankles as he was forced into playing in what at times was the unfamiliar position of left-back. One or two boos echoed around the stadium. The Dips were winning, but their defensive tactics weren't appreciated by some who no doubt showed up expecting to see blood and thunder – where was it? The only thing the Dips cared about was seeing out the game. Pelé was lucky to stay on the field, throwing a left hook at the Dips' Mike Lester, but as Eric Martin said,

'The ref couldn't send Pelé off – everyone had come to see him play.'

There was a riot for Pelé's shirt after the game. Perhaps the Cosmos management forgot to substitute him shortly before the final whistle in order to give him the opportunity to slink away to the safety of the away team dressing room. Or perhaps they just enjoyed the sight of the world's most famous footballer being hunted down like a dog by a bunch of hangers-on and Dips players.

But like the wily old campaigner he was, Pelé ripped off his jersey and threw it one way before sprinting away in the other direction. It was left to two of Bobby's playing colleagues to charge after it like opponents in a game of rugby trying to reach the ball first on the try line. There they wrestled one another for their stake on a piece of memorabilia. Bobby was far away from the circus.

Pelé went on to lead New York Cosmos to the Soccer Bowl. They beat Tampa Bay Rowdies, Fort Lauderdale Strikers and Rochester Lancers on the way to the final in Portland where they beat Seattle Sounders. This meant that Bobby, along with Jim and Eric Martin, were part of the last team to beat Pelé in a competitive football match. Thankfully, it wasn't Bobby's last game. Two weeks later he made his Portsmouth debut in Gosport.

16

My Local Pompey

THE only thing Portsmouth had to pay out for Bobby was the postage for sending his registration papers to the Football League by express delivery. They wanted him in a hurry. On the Friday morning before their game with Peterborough, manager Jimmy Dickinson telephoned the Football League from the team hotel to make sure Bobby's registration papers had arrived.

It was August 1977. He'd been back in town for 11 days having spent the summer playing for Washington in the North American Soccer League, which wasn't due to start again until April. Once again, Portsmouth were operating on a shoestring budget. Bobby was a free agent – this was the end of the market they did their business in. It wasn't the only offer on the table – Fourth Division Bournemouth threw their hat into the ring. Not only were they prepared to pay, they went to the newspapers claiming that their deal was good and Bobby was keen on joining them. It didn't materialise and Bobby went to Fratton Park.

It was on his doorstep and the team he had referred to in his post-FA Cup Final interview as 'my local Pompey'.

It was also a case of third time lucky. The club turned him down as teenager in the 1960s, then he decided against joining them in 1975; now he was finally signing up for his home-town team. First Portsmouth got clearance from the Football Association, via the NASL, for Bobby to play for an English club. Then all they had to do was fill out the paperwork. Still, Bobby was anxious. It was the waiting, the not knowing. It was the teamsheet pinned up at The Dell on a Friday all over again.

Bobby opened up, telling the local press he was delighted to be a Pompey player. 'They've always been something a bit special with me. It's been dreadful waiting for things to be cleared up, now I can't wait to get playing again,' he said, choosing to overlook the fact he was about to begin his 12th consecutive month playing football. This prolonged season began at Wembley when playing for Southampton in the Charity Shield in August of 1976 and looked set to continue for Portsmouth in the Third Division through the winter of 1978.

He had hopes – he wanted to do a good job – it was his team. He also wanted the time to bed in and get accustomed to his new, albeit familiar surroundings. Yes, the piss-taking in the dressing room would be the same the world over and he'd have no problem falling into that groove. It was the style and ability of the team he wanted to adapt to. 'I hope I can do a job for Pompey wherever they want me to play,' he said. 'But I hope people will give me a chance to settle in and get to know the other lads and how they play.'

That was the club's intention, too. Jimmy had been content to wait until the following week to chase up Bobby's registration. Bed him in slowly, let him get a gradual feel for what it meant to be a Portsmouth player. It didn't quite turn out that way though. There wasn't the time for settling in, for players or managers. Ian St

John, who wanted Bobby to come to Fratton Park less than two years beforehand, had been relieved of his duties. Jimmy Dickinson was in charge now, having kept Portsmouth in Division Three the previous season. Jimmy was Mr Portsmouth. Although long gone, his memory is commemorated in the form of a mural of his face on the seats of the Fratton End, which is home to the more vociferous contingent of Portsmouth supporters. It's said that Jim was never booked. It would explain the nickname Gentleman Jim, but no bookings? Not once in the 700-odd games he played for Portsmouth? Not in the glory years of back-to-back league titles or the later days when the club were relegated to the Second Division? Did he have ice running through his veins?

Previously he'd worked for the club in public relations. Those skills would some in handy, but he didn't have to take the job. It put his reputation on the line, potentially leading to a situation whereby fans would want him to leave. Jimmy had said there was no need to rush Bobby in for the Peterborough game. Injury scares to Clive Green and Maitland Pollock changed his mind, worrying the club into chasing up his paperwork – they needed to take 12 players to London Road. The Football League confirmed the paperwork had arrived in sufficient time, meaning Bobby was eligible to play. He didn't, though. He sat the game out from the bench and watched his new team-mates play out a scoreless draw. This game demonstrated where Portsmouth were at in 1977. Jimmy said he'd toyed several times with the idea of throwing Bobby on in the second half. Maybe he would have provided the difference in a game that was noted for its absence of flair. But Jimmy was too preoccupied with caution. He was concerned a substitution might upset the rhythm of the team. It seemed as though that rhythm constituted little more than snuffing out the opposition's attacks. Maybe it was a day for rolled-up sleeves. Jimmy couldn't see them losing; he wasn't prepared to gamble for a win. 'Bobby could, of course, have come on and scored and that would have been tremendous,' said Jimmy. 'But if things had gone the other way people would have wanted to know why I upset things.'

The two points allocated for a win back in 1977 did not promote a gung-ho approach, especially away from home. Why go for the throat when you could go for the draw? The local press seemed content. A 0-0 draw at Peterborough might not have set pulses racing at many other clubs, but this was Portsmouth – who had lost their four opening games of the season. Long-time *Portsmouth News* journalist Mike Neasom seemed to sense the hardship that would follow for the club when he wrote in his report that everyone must hope that the start would augur well for the nine months to come. It didn't, of course.

It's not that Jimmy doubted Bobby. He was confident Bobby would do a good job for the club. But what exactly did that mean? Bobby was a good player – he'd played and scored goals in the First Division. This didn't mean he could walk into the team and go on mazy runs past the opposition's entire defence. That wasn't his game either. It didn't matter if it was a division below what he'd been used to. He had forged pretty good working relationships with Mick Channon and Peter Osgood. Each one knew what the other could and could not do. But aside from all the bluster about Bobby needing time to settle in, it wouldn't have been unreasonable for Portsmouth fans to expect him to impose himself on the team – use his experience to manage games on the field of play.

He didn't have to wait long for his debut, which came on a Monday night in a friendly with Hampshire League champions Gosport Borough at Privett Park. Portsmouth fielded a full-strength team and Bobby scored. He made his league debut at against Swindon Town before scoring at Fratton Park against Chesterfield while playing in a deeper midfield role. The match reports were still critical of his performance, as they felt Bobby lacked sharpness and struggled to make things tick. This sluggishness was no doubt due to 14 months of non-stop football. When asked about his goal, a powerful strike, Bobby was self-effacing as ever, 'I had to do something right, didn't I.'

Today, Dave Kemp is Tony Pulis's right-hand man, having worked with him at Stoke City, Crystal Palace and now West Bromwich Albion. But back then Dave was very much Portsmouth's shining light. He rated Bobby. He just didn't think he commanded things on the field for Portsmouth as much as he'd have expected in terms of belief in his ability as a footballer, especially for somebody who scored the winner in a cup final. 'Bobby was very unassuming,' said Dave. 'If I'd scored the winner in the cup final you'd never get me to shut up.' The opposite was true of Bobby.

The club's fans were starting to lose their patience. They'd been served up promises for too long. They don't look back on the 1977/78 season with any affection. Some say it was the poorest Portsmouth team in living memory. Others joke the team had players in it that Pompey supporters wouldn't cross the road to spit on. Both statements need to be put into context – Portsmouth had no money. They were also always on the lookout for players, but were usually put off by the transfer fees. They went after Sheffield United's Dennis Longhorn, but the reported fee of £25,000 was beyond their means. So they had to throw a lot of youngsters in the first team in a physically demanding league in front of frustrated fans. Being a former Southampton player might have been baggage you could have done without at Fratton Park. Players took the brunt of criticism – Bobby took his fair share, but such harsh judgement wasn't lost on him – he was often his own harshest critic. Portsmouth may have been his local team, but the boyhood dream was quickly turning into a nightmare.

17

Tough Crowd

BOBBY walked out on to Portsmouth's training pitch at Eastney Barracks with the golden boot he won for Southampton. This wasn't provocation, it was a favour for his new team-mates. 'The lads cajoled him into it,' said Peter Denyer, one of several youngsters in the Portsmouth squad during the 1977/78 season. Without their persistence Bobby would never have brought that boot into training. 'We all got a chance to hold it,' said Peter. 'We were passing it around and asking Bobby if he drank beer out of it during the FA Cup Final celebrations – Bobby said we could drink beer out of it now if we liked.'

It was another example of how the rivalry between the two south coast clubs stopped on the terraces. The idea an artefact so intrinsically linked with Southampton's finest hour was being passed around by Portsmouth players with the giddy excitement of schoolchildren would be too much for many Portsmouth fans to stomach. But it happened. The jury may have been out when it came to the Portsmouth fans, but Bobby was popular with his new team-mates. Peter admitted to being in awe of Bobby when he

156

first arrived. He was there at Wembley when Southampton won the cup at Wembley, not as some surreptitious Southampton supporter, but as a fan of the game. He was one of few who took up the option all professional footballers had in obtaining a cup final ticket, committing to going before he knew who'd be contesting the final.

Peter felt it was a great chance to watch a big game and learn from it. He remembers Bobby as a positive person with a smile on his face, who was always taking the mick. 'I was just soaking it all in,' said Peter. 'I think Bobby was happy to take the accolades that the cup final goal provided him, but it was like the winner's medal and the golden boot themselves didn't mean a great deal to him.' Bobby's move to Fratton Park had come as a bit of a surprise to former Portsmouth midfielder Norman Piper. Norman played for Portsmouth for eight years during the 1970s, but has spent the best part of the last 40 years living in the States, where he works as a soccer coach. He still returns to Portsmouth from time to time. Spending so much time on the other side of the pond has done nothing to diminish his understanding of the rivalry between the two clubs. He recalls watching a Southampton match on TV a few years back. 'The other team's fans started singing "Play up Pompey" to get the Saints' fans backs up,' he laughed. 'That's a rivalry, man – it's funny.'

Norman played in the local derby when the two clubs found themselves together in the Second Division between 1974 and 1976. Bobby played in all four of the league games. Southampton won all of them, including the victory at Fratton Park on Boxing Day 1974 and the last-minute goal by Mick Channon which effectively sent Portsmouth down to the Third Division in April 1976. They were big games. The support factor some Portsmouth fans claimed rang true. The derby attendance at Fratton Park was higher than it was at The Dell in 1974, but only by 173 people – as the gates hit the 19,000 mark. There was a bigger gulf in figures during the 1975/76 season. While around 24,000 fans filled Fratton Park three days after Southampton had won their FA Cup semi-final, only a little over 17,000 were at The Dell for the earlier fixture in September. If this was due to indifference because of a second successive season in Division Two then maybe those Portsmouth fans had a point, but Southampton were able to draw crowds at The Dell of over 20,000, with 27,000 there to see off West Bromwich Albion in the FA Cup quarter-final replay. This was understandable though – what club wouldn't pull in a big attendance when the carrot of an FA Cup semi-final dangled in front of them?

That's not to say the derby wasn't of great importance. 'Nervous? Sure,' said Norman. 'If you're not nervous going into a game like that you shouldn't be playing. But once you're out there knocking a ball around it's fine.' Norman draws a distinct line between how fans and players see the game. 'Players don't care about the rivalry though. It's the fans that make it. Some of us used to go up Salisbury races with the Southampton players – Peter Osgood, Alan Ball, Mick Channon. You'd have a drink afterwards. It'd be like "We're going to Salisbury on Tuesday, wanna come?" "Yeah, sure." You're enemies on the field, but afterwards we'll have a drink – we're all in this together as professionals.'

Fans choose to ignore this. The idea of players of rival clubs cosying up to one another did not in any way fit the narrative on the terraces, which basically followed the line that the other was to be hated at all costs. Norman felt Bobby and Paul were accepted by the Fratton Park crowd. 'The fans understood we needed players,' said Norman. 'Bobby used to play with a smile on his face – the game's missing that now. And while you get nervous before a game the fans at Fratton Park were always unbelievable –

they could really get behind you.' Norman recalls training being more intense under Ian St John than it was under Jimmy Dickinson. 'Ian would say it how it is. But if you're gonna do well you need good players, doesn't matter who the coach is. And we were struggling for players.'

It was true. The Fratton Park crowd could get behind you. Elements of it could also paralyse, Maitland Pollock will tell you that. A Scot, better known down south as Matt Pollock, mainly because Harry Haslam, his boss at Luton Town, told him that the name Maitland would never catch on among his colleagues, dismissing Mait – his real name's shortened version and one of the most popular terms in football language, albeit with a different spelling. Maitland was a self confessed St John man, 'I would've run through a brick wall for him.' So it's no surprise that he thinks Dickinson was simply not as tactically aware as St John. 'Dickinson had been out of the game for a while when he became manager,' said Maitland, dismissing Dickinson's involvement with the club's public relations. He found Dickinson's man-management skills peculiar. Maitland was not somebody who could keep his feelings to himself, and he had his run-ins with Jimmy. 'I'd go to his office and speak my mind. His wife was in the office once. I told him what I have to say is between me and you and he said, "You want my wife to leave?" Yes, I do.'

Bobby appeared very laid back from where Maitland was standing. 'Nothing ever seemed to phase him,' said Maitland, who recognised Bobby had good skill, but he had doubts about his fitness in terms of ability to get about the field. 'At times he seemed maybe a yard short of pace. I often wondered if his laid-back attitude came out somehow in his play.' This is the polar opposite of what his colleagues at Southampton would say – fitness was what Bobby was all about. Was the suggestion that Bobby was past his best? Not at 26, surely. It's more likely his time at

Fratton Park was hampered by being knackered from no breaks from playing for an entire year.

Having spent 1976/77 with Southampton, Bobby had gone straight into a full season in Washington during the summer, where temperatures would average 30 degrees Celsius. The heat was one thing, but the high humidity meant games would drain energy. Former Washington Diplomat Alan Green would agree with this. When he returned from the summer NASL season to play for Coventry City he was given three weeks off. He hadn't asked for it – management decreed he needed it having burnt himself out from playing continuously through winter and summer.

No doubt Bobby would have benefited from a rest. It wasn't a luxury he had at Portsmouth. They needed everybody they could find. Having once had his knee in plaster, Maitland found himself on the bench two weeks after taking it off. It wasn't ideal to be thrown back in but there was no money for new players. It was not a happy period for Bobby. Pockets of vocal support would save their more sarcastic comments for him. Having lost control of what seemed the simplest of passes, someone punctuated the groans by shouting, 'Still dreaming about the cup final, Stokes?' It summed things up and it was humiliating. Footballers develop a thick enough skin to deal with criticism from their own fans, but this cut deeper. It was a special kind of nihilism on show, with fans prepared to have a laugh at Bobby's expense even if the punchline around that joke was actually at the expense of their own team. After a while Maria Johnson stopped going to Fratton Park to watch her cousin play. 'I didn't like it if he got shouted at,' she said. 'I'm no fighter, but I could have punched them for some of the things they said.'

'Fans pay their money, so they deserve to have their say,' said Maitland. 'It's just that sometimes some fans don't always give the most educated opinions.' Portsmouth fans like to say they never get on the back of their own. Not always true. It could be brutal at Fratton Park. One Portsmouth fan in particular seemed to have it in for Maitland, giving him all sorts of abuse every time he touched the ball. Then one week an unusual opportunity arose to get his own back, as a slide tackle near the touchline provided him with the momentum to take him over the barrier and into the stand. 'In a split second I could see I was about to collide with someone – it was him. In a second, I put my arm across his neck and just whispered in his ear, "Not another word from you, son." And that was that.'

A whispered threat carries more weight when said in a Scottish accent. It seemed to do the trick and Maitland never heard from him again. Although Maitland took his fair share of criticism from Portsmouth fans, he felt at times it was justified, 'I was playing out on the left, but I was trying too hard. St John ended up sticking me up front with Dave Kemp. It worked.' Reporter Mike Neasom profiled Maitland in the *Portsmouth News*, 'He called me the cheerful chaser, that's what I did, and I earned respect.' If nothing else, the fans wanted to see players working up a sweat for the cause.

Peter Denyer believes that fans paid their money so they were free to voice their opinion. 'Sometimes you could hear individual criticism aimed at you,' said Peter. 'It could affect you in different ways, depending on how the game was going. It's not as simple as getting stick meant you played badly. You might be carrying confidence from a goal, or you might not be getting the ball.' Although one thing Peter agrees on is that if given a choice he'd rather not experience it.

Ray Crawford was Jimmy's assistant. Born and bred in Portsmouth, he played for the club before making his name as a goalscorer in Alf Ramsey's title-winning Ipswich Town side of 1961. 'You have to win the fans over at Fratton Park,' said Ray. 'It doesn't matter where you're from – Alan McLoughlin showed that when he moved from Southampton to Portsmouth.' McLoughlin became popular at Fratton Park, but his stay at The Dell was short-lived. Southampton may have broken their transfer record by paying £700,000 up front, but he was never accommodated in his true position of just behind the front two so Southampton fans didn't see enough of him before he moved on a little over a year after signing.

Ray, who knew what it was like to be an important player, is more generous than some when assessing Bobby's spell at Fratton Park. 'Bobby was a good player,' insisted Ray. 'Maybe a few steps ahead of the other boys a lot of the time. I remember Lawrie McMenemy saying, "Bobby was a lad who liked a game of football, a game of darts and a beer." That was Bobby. In the end it was a bad move for him, but he couldn't say no at the time – not to his home club.' Ray has similar first-hand experience, going back to Ipswich later in his career, 'People said I was mad when I went back, but it worked, but you need a bit of luck.' Ray doesn't think Bobby got that. 'Bobby trained hard and gave everything for me, but it was a raw and inexperienced team.'

Paul Gilchrist's memories are less happy. He was aware of the rivalry between the two teams having played in the derby for Southampton, but he wanted to play first-team football after being frozen out at The Dell. Ian St John offered him the chance to do so at Portsmouth but Paul's experience is indicative of how things were at Fratton Park at the time. Having moved to Titchfield, a village situated between the cities, Portsmouth offered to pay Paul's legal fees on his new house. He was then later chased as the fees weren't paid. By this time St John had been sacked and there didn't seem to have been anyone keeping their eyes on that part of Paul's contract.

It didn't get much better on the field for Paul, who was singled out by Portsmouth fans. 'I was booed during the warm-up, which was lovely,' said Paul, who clearly recalls an away match at Lincoln. 'Around an hour before kick-off I went out with Dave Kemp to check the turf – the fans saw him and cheered, they saw me and booed.' There were a little over 4,000 people at Sincil Bank on that cold February afternoon and the mood was not good.

Paul cannot remember if Bobby got booed for his Southampton connections. 'If you were an asset to the club then you'd be accepted, but if you struggled you were singled out.' Bobby played in a friendly against Fort Lauderdale the week after the 1-0 defeat at Lincoln – it was his last appearance before heading back to Washington to fulfil his contractual obligations with the Diplomats. He was on the winning side for Portsmouth three times in his 24 league appearances.

Southampton ended their 1977/78 Second Division season with promotion, nestled a point ahead of Spurs and a point behind champions Bolton. Portsmouth finished rock bottom of the Third Division. Bobby wouldn't be asked back. 'I'm the first to admit that my time here has been a disaster,' said Bobby. 'I hoped I might provide the spark Pompey needed and I haven't.' He would later return to Portsmouth, but not as a footballer.

18

Get Your Kicks

BOBBY liked Washington – he said it reminded him of home. The suggestion sounded preposterous. His home city of Portsmouth, the place he left in March 1978, was a frozen wasteland, with the atmosphere at Fratton Park equally caustic. Portsmouth were relegated to the Fourth Division shortly after Bobby flew back to the US for the 1978 season with the Diplomats.

Life in the US was the perfect antidote for any grief he received from some sections of the crowd during his truncated spell with Pompey. Not everything was to his liking though. Bobby hated flying. So did Tommy O'Hara, a Scot who joined Washington from Queen of the South. This was a problem when playing in a league which required extensive air travel. The two first met during a tour of the Dominican Republic. So what did they have in common? 'We both liked a beer,' said Tommy. 'You know, Bobby was content with a beer and a smoke – his wife would look after the bills and that kind of thing.'

Bobby's nickname for Tommy summed up the dry sense of humour he was known for. 'He'd always call me

"Bagpipe",' said Tommy, who had his own nickname for Bobby. 'That accent of his was like lots of English people,' said Tommy. 'Bobby missed out his Hs, so I called him an "Ampshire Og".' The pair invented ways to take their minds off of the constant air travel. 'We used to get the *Sporting Life* newspaper sent over from the UK,' said Tommy. 'During plane journeys we'd sit and pick winners, betting against ourselves.'

There was no real bet placed on any horse, the outcome of the race having long been decided by the time they received the paper. The thrill was simply in checking the results. But checking the racing results wasn't always enough to distract them from the perils of flying. The club would help the pair take their minds off it and everything else. 'They'd give us these pills,' said Tommy. 'We'd take them in the airport bar and knock them back with a few Millers. It'd knock us out cold by the time we got on the plane.'

The mindset to the game in the States was pretty well summed up by Washington Diplomats' 1978 promotional video, 'Soccer is a game that truly reflects contemporary society – constant movement, constant excitement and constant frustration.' Constant promotion too; football was promoted much more aggressively in the US back then than it ever was in the UK, but it had to be. The game was competing for attention against a host of other far more established sports so you had a scenario where players were effectively employed as footballers, as well as missionaries, who went out into the community to spread the word about the game. The end result being they'd hopefully get a few more bums on seats come matchday.

Clubs in the North American Soccer League were prepared to go to extremes when it came to spreading that word. Dips goalkeeper Eric Martin once rode an elephant through the streets of Washington into RFK stadium in the name of soccer. How exactly that event translated to gate receipts is unknown, but put simply the NASL was prepared to do whatever it could to generate interest in the game.

Much of Washington's marketing focused on the good standard of facilities fans could enjoy on matchday. This wasn't wrong. RFK stadium was light years ahead of The Dell and Fratton Park. Those two venues were football grounds, while RFK was a proper sports venue, capable of seating more than 55,000 people or a sold-out performance by The Rolling Stones. These are the kind of crowds that the Washington Redskins, the city's American football team, could draw in 1978. The Dips were still effectively only four years old so they were still building a fan-base. The biggest crowd they had in 1978 was 17,000 for the visit of New York Cosmos. Once again, the Dips were chasing their New York counterparts' coat-tails in the Eastern Division of the National Conference.

By this time Dips goalkeeper Eric Martin had suffered a broken leg which ended his career. His replacement, Bill Irwin, is a softly-spoken Irishman who made his way to the Diplomats via Cardiff City. He recalls the team enjoying a more laid-back atmosphere than in the UK. 'Fans were mainly families, so it was a gentler atmosphere than what you'd get at home,' said Bill. Sadly, many will know from bitter experience that the presence of women and children isn't always enough to prevent everyone from jumping out their seat to use abusive language. But that kind of behaviour didn't tend to happen in the NASL. The less aggressive nature of the fans wasn't to suggest the stadiums were packed full of novices asking what the offside rule was, because Bill remembers there being many knowledgeable fans. That said, the country as a whole was still learning about the game. 'So if you did make a mistake,' said Bill, 'you knew you wouldn't get crucified by the fans for it.'

There were no travelling fans either. The idea of fans travelling the 2,000-plus miles for an away game with Seattle Sounders was too far-fetched and therefore there was no need for segregation and no fan trouble. That's not to say players were on holiday from responsibility. Bill recalls the club owners expected the team to reach the play-offs. But they also knew they needed to draw in a regular and larger fan-base. The promotional video was prepared to lay it on thick when it came to describing what soccer represented in the US, 'The Washington Diplomats have brought professional soccer's renaissance to the nation's capital. Now kids from all over the area dream of a day they can enter a giant arena to hear thousands cheers as they kick a winning goal for the Dips – so come on and get your kicks with the Dips.' Cue the music, an elongated jingle which features the vocal, 'Get your kicks, with the Dips.'

Viewers are then given behind the scenes access as Dips coach Gordon Bradley gives his pre-match team talk. Even the changing rooms look to be superior to what would have been on offer in the UK; far more roomy, and also appearing to be carpeted, with each player having his own chair and cubicle. This was verging on decadence when compared to the idea of an entire team sharing one giant bath together, like they did in the UK, the plug clogging up with mud and other gunk. Gordon comes across like the archetypal PE teacher addressing a sixth-form rugby team when he says, 'I want to see 100 per cent effort, great attitude and a will to win – let's see if we can be top of the league tonight.' The nature of the video makes you wonder if this was all staged just for the promotional film. It makes sense. When aiming for a new, family-orientated audience, it is probably not ideal to have the hard sell peppered with expletives.

So if this film was part of the club's big sell to potential new fans, where did Bobby fit into it all? The answer is quite highly in the pecking order. The video introduces 'number 25, Dips' dynamite striker Bobby Stokes'. It ends with a goal from Bobby against Chicago Sting. He was playing in the future. It was everything the English Premier League adopted 20 years down the line and more. Shin pads were optional, players had their name printed on the back of their shirt and some wore white boots. They had been seen in the 1970s but were a very rare occurrence. Bobby had little choice when it came to footwear as the decision was made by the club's general manager John Carbray. 'He cut some kind of deal with Adidas,' said Bill. 'From then on we had to wear white Adidas cleats with the blue and red stripes. If you didn't wear them you'd be fined a week's wages.'

There were further features of the matchday experience in Washington that would send a shiver down the spine of the football purist. The centre circle at RFK was spray-painted with a giant mural of a football, just in case anyone was in any doubt or needed reminding of the exact sport they were watching. They even dyed the penalty areas red to emphasise the area in which the goalkeeper could handle the ball.

Bill used to pick Bobby up for training in his Chevy Nova. They'd be joined by fellow Brits Mike Dillon and Tommy O'Hara in a car which was always filled with the chatter of four young men engaging in for want of a better phrase, plenty of piss-taking. They'd drive to RFK and get changed, but they didn't train on the stadium's pitch. 'As a soccer team we were very much second-class citizens,' said Steve Horner, who was the Dips' physiotherapist. 'No way would we be allowed to use the RFK pitch. At first we trained on the polo grounds – which wasn't great for obvious reasons, it had had horses stomping all over it, and then we used the military grounds. At RFK we trained on a field adjacent to the stadium parking lot. It was usually used for fan parking on NFL games. At times it was a bit bumpy and a bit hard to train on.' The local park training vibe wasn't much different from what the UK-based players were used to at home; after all, Bobby joined a Southampton team that sometimes trained on the car park. It wasn't going to be a problem for him.

'Bobby had a nose for goal,' said Bill. 'If he put one past you in training he'd rub it in – let you know about it for a few days.' Maybe Bobby would put one in the bottom corner of Bill's goal, walking back across the parking lot to get changed teasing Bill, saying, 'Where were you, Bill?' He would still be on the subject after they showered and changed and got back into Bill's car. All that mickey-taking about a goal or two scored on a pitch that doubled up as a parking lot during big games, but not a word ever mentioned about the goal he scored in the FA Cup Final. 'You'd have to prise it out of him,' added Bill. 'He never brought it up – I think he had his winner's medal tucked away somewhere in a bank box. Not like Steeley [Jim Steele], who'd wear his around his neck. Not to say Jim was a boaster, just how he was. We're all different.'

The Dips qualified for the 1978 NASL play-offs, but Bobby's last-minute equaliser couldn't stop them from eventually losing in overtime against Portland Timbers. He returned to the UK for the winter without playing for anybody and when he returned to the US with the Dips in 1979 he went on a long scoreless run before he showed that nose for goal once more. The 16 games he went without finding the net were more to do with his responsibilities in a deeper-lying midfield role, but his old colleagues still saw him as an attacking player.

Mike Dillon arrived at the Dips via Tottenham Hotspur and New York Cosmos. 'Bobby was a bit like an old-fashioned inside-forward,' said Mike. 'He'd hold players off and want the ball played into his feet.' General manager

John Carbray was more succinct when he described Bobby as the most underrated player on the team.

Not long after that, Bobby scored a hat-trick against Tampa Bay Rowdies, who were no pushovers, later reaching the 1979 Soccer Bowl. Bobby felt redemption. 'The first goal took an awful lot of weight off me,' he said. 'When you're having a bad time a change is often welcome. I felt relaxed and confident up there. But it's the breaks of the game. It could easily have been Paul in those spots. Who knows?' The Paul he was referring to was the Geordie striker and renowned playboy Paul Cannell, whose larger-than-life personality could have just as easily walked off the set of the film *Anchorman*. Cannell was dropped and Bobby was the hero, or at least that was the gist. His philosophy about the breaks of the game suggested life was a game of chance and the pendulum had simply once more swung his way, as opposed to him having taken advantage of those breaks by taking life by the short and curlies.

Mike Dillon spent plenty of time on the road with Bobby, noticing he didn't always seem too worried about looking after himself, 'We'd get food at the hotel, and sometimes he'd just pick at his plate before pushing it to one side and having a smoke instead.' Getting his five a day may not have been on the top of his agenda, but his hair remained resplendent, cascading over his ears like gossamer. He took pride over his appearance. 'Bobby was the only guy I've ever known to have a shower and wash his hair before the game,' added Mike. Bobby scored in the 1979 play-offs against Los Angeles Aztecs, but once again it was in vain as the Dips lost the deciding game 4-3.

A chance encounter with Terry Paine on Bobby's return home, at a wedding in Waterlooville, resulted in him playing a chunk of the 1979/80 season at Cheltenham Town, who Terry was managing while running a pub around the corner from their ground in Medway Road.

He paid Bobby something like £45 per game. Bobby had a sideline though. 'He sold a lot of sheepskin coats,' said Terry. 'Good ones too – I had one.' Terry has no idea where the coats came from and he never asked.

Cheltenham played in the Southern League, with never more than 1,000 people watching games and sometimes less than 100. If their paths hadn't have crossed at that wedding it's unlikely that Bobby would have played football during 1979/80. Bobby began that season aged 28, which in hindsight comes as a surprise to Terry Paine. Like so many things where Bobby was concerned the reality wasn't always in keeping with the commonly held belief.

19

American Highway

LEATHER slippers and the absence of a football didn't prevent Ray Graydon demonstrating how to take the perfect penalty. Stood in his conservatory, Ray ran through his technique while I sat on the sofa in front of him acting as a hypothetical goalkeeper. He roomed with Bobby when the two played together for Washington Diplomats in 1978, meaning they spent plenty of time together. 'I'd ask Bobby about his football. He told me that Steeley, Osgood and Channon always looked after him,' said Ray. 'It seemed a strange thing to say at first. I don't think I've ever said that to anybody. You might get on well with a team-mate, but I could never imagine saying that I relied on another player to look after me. You've got to sort yourself out – what if that person left? Perhaps that's why he would ask me what I thought?'

It was as though Bobby was looking to Ray for guidance. Ray was happy to provide it. The future coach and manager in him revealed a methodical man, whose analysis was very much underpinned by common sense. He was good company for Bobby, he could reassure any

172

doubts over his form and back it up with reason. 'Bobby would say something like, "Do you think I'm getting enough of the ball? When I'm showing on the right should I be getting the ball?" I'd tell him he needed to speak to whoever was playing full-back. He should have told him he needed two minutes with them, that he needed the ball to feet, not smacked over the top.'

Bobby would nod. But the confidence Ray spoke of was that of a coach, of a senior figure. Bobby wasn't able to see himself like that. Ray thought Bobby was a better player than he was given credit for. 'In terms of playing style I compare him to Jermain Defoe – he had a short backlift when striking the ball. He could pick a pass and had a strong will to win,' said Ray, who has something else in common with Bobby: he too scored the winning goal in a cup final. Ray's came from the penalty spot for Aston Villa in the 1975 League Cup showpiece. He often took penalties and wasn't put off by failing to convert one on the odd occasion. Good job, too, as his initial penalty at Wembley was pushed on to the post before he showed the sufficient composure to poke home the rebound.

Ray's penalty success was born out of hours of practice, and he now says, 'When I hear England haven't been practising penalties I think what the hell have they been doing?' The exasperation in his voice is due to England's poor record in penalty shoot-outs not being countered by thorough preparation. That isn't something Ray could be accused of in his playing, coaching and management career, and he says, 'There are few people in the world who could get away without really practising.'

Ray thinks Matt Le Tissier was one of them. Ray brought Matt to Oxford United on trial when he worked as the club's youth team coach, getting him accommodation at his wife's accountant's house. So in a parallel universe Le Tissier could have been specialising in spectacular goals at

Oxford's old Manor Ground, but having been brought up in Guernsey he struggled to settle on the mainland away from his family. Ray later coached him at Southampton. Matt was an expert penalty-taker, only missing once from the spot in his entire career, but Ray took a dim view of his approach to practising penalties back then in the 1980s and told him so.

'But Matt's penalty record cannot be criticised,' said Ray, who believes there needs to be a clear strategy when taking spot-kicks. 'After taking God knows how many penalties in training I found that striking with the instep was best. I ended up with a technique I think is best and most reliable percentage-wise.' He stepped up to strike his imaginary ball with the instep of his right foot, before asking, 'What am I doing with my body when I'm doing that?' He was shaping up. 'Exactly – I'm running up to the ball at a 45-degree angle, so where am I going to put the ball?' I suggested that it would be going to my left. 'Yes, it could go there, but I could also wrap my foot around the ball and drill it into the keeper's bottom-right corner.' Ray said that it is the best way to go without the keeper knowing where to dive. 'If you hit it just inside the post at a good pace then it's got a 99.9 per cent chance of going in.'

Ray's clear instructions make it very easy to imagine him working as a coach. But back in 1978 he was still a player and playing football in the US was a great opportunity, albeit one which was offset with plenty of time spent sat waiting around in airport lounges in New England to San Diego, Fort Lauderdale to Vancouver. Travel is an inevitable part of a footballer's job but it was relentless in the States. It wasn't unusual for the Dips to go on five-day trips which covered two cities and five separate flights.

The challenge is what you do with the time at your disposal. Ray never found the travel enjoyable in England, let alone the States, sat on a coach going from one spot to another to play a game of football. 'I'd sit quietly, have a chat, maybe have a game of cards,' he said. 'But I could see it being a bit of a problem for Bobby – he'd needed to be out with the lads.'

The last trip Ray went on with Bobby was to Korea, for the President's Cup. It was an invitational tournament organised by the Korean Football Association. It was a strange mix. South Korea, Sao Paulo's under-21 side, Eintracht Frankfurt, Pas Tehran and the Lebanese national team all joined Washington Diplomats in a 24-team tournament in September. It was a long-haul flight, stopping off on the US west coast and then Hawaii before making its way to Seoul in South Korea. Sleeping pills weren't strong enough for this journey and Ray remembers Bobby needing to drink on the plane to calm his nerves.

It wasn't just the travel itself that was the problem. There was plenty of other time to kill on the trip. Ray remembers playing a lot of tennis with Dips goalkeeper Bill Irwin. 'Bobby wouldn't have been interested in doing that,' said Ray, who still thinks about Bobby. Sometimes he goes for a pint – sometimes in the day, something he never used to dream of doing; but he's retired now after a long career in football and he's enjoying it, too. 'I get the bus back after a couple of beers and think, "What would Bob be doing?" He'd be there at the bar – it's a pity Bobby's not still around to enjoy life.'

Ray got the impression Bobby thought he was a bit of a stuffed shirt when they first met. This changed when the two were assigned community work together, involving coaching women. The women's game was not yet what it was soon to develop into in the US and the coaching session Ray and Bobby had been assigned to was a bit of a publicity stunt. 'It's as though they'd picked the girls purely on their looks and nothing else – they were like a bunch of Miss Worlds,' said Ray, who was looking to get into coaching and Bobby was happy to help as long as it was clear that Ray would lead the session.

Ray began a series of drills. After it became clear none of the young women were able to perform the majority of them, Ray tried something simpler, involving controlling the ball on the chest, which Ray, having had the previous 20 minutes or so to test the atmosphere, casually referred to as the 'booby trap'. 'I mean, I'd get hauled over the coals for saying something like that today,' said Ray. 'It's inappropriate, but the girls thought it was funny – Bobby thought it was hysterical.' From then on he was more relaxed in Ray's company.

The difference between the pair's cup final achievements is that Ray's ranks alongside many others. Aston Villa have won many trophies – Ray won the League Cup again with the club before they famously won the European Cup in 1982, having won the league title the year before. Not that these other achievements stop Ray getting asked about his winning goal in 1975. So what is it like to say you've scored the winning goal in a cup final at Wembley? It must be a great feeling? 'It is,' smiled Ray. 'I've said it a million times. And that's something Bob's missing because he's not with us. Very often somebody will come up to me and say, "My dad never stops talking about you." It's never them – always their dads,' Ray laughs. His winning cup final goal was more than 40 years ago now.

Fans don't just want to talk to Ray – his goal goes beyond that. He remembers receiving a letter from a supporter shortly after he left Villa Park. 'It was a lovely letter,' said Ray. 'It was all about what the cup final meant to him.' The writer wanted to let Ray know that he planned to name his son Graydon. Ray looked bemused. 'Graydon?' he said. 'What sort of flipping name is that to give anybody?' The writer has been in touch with Ray many times over the years and has written several books about Aston Villa. So in some ways, Ray's success has spurred others on to achieve. Through his goal Ray has become part of other people's lives. Apparently there are several others named after him. Whether or not there was a surge in the number of boys called Robert in Southampton in 1976, in honour of Bobby, remains unclear. What is easier to appreciate is that scoring a goal of such magnitude brought with it a very personal legacy. It wasn't reduced to simply a place in the pages of the history books, it meant a place in the hearts and minds of the people who supported that team.

'I can't remember anyone not liking Bobby,' said Ray. 'That's quite something. There'd be quite a few people who would say they didn't like me. Maybe they found me grating, or if I wanted something done as a coach they'd think I was stubborn. Not with Stokesy. No one would ever say, oh idiot or big head. Never. It was more than that though.' Ray scratched his head before choosing the right phrase. 'Bobby was likeable – not full-on about himself, which is a nice thing. But you probably need a bit of that in football. In football terms you must have confidence in your abilities – being cocky can be okay if you know how to handle it and not go over the top. It wasn't until I was 26 or 27 that I really thought I knew what I was doing as a professional footballer.

'Before that I was a bit apprehensive at times; lacing my boots before a game hoping I had a good day. After that though I knew my job – I couldn't guarantee I'd score goals, but I knew how to make it difficult for the full-back I was up against. I knew the job – that gives you confidence. But Bob never gave me the impression he had that inner confidence, ever.'

The manager in Ray was weighing up his team-mate, but trying to instil belief in him was not straightforward. 'I liked Bobby as a person,' said Ray. 'He wasn't a moaner

– he had a chuckle. Maybe sometimes he'd get down, but I'd try not to let him get down.' Life on the road could grind you down. Occasionally Ray would notice Bobby repetitively checking that the hotel door was locked at night. 'I'd say, flipping hell, Bobby – don't worry about that.' But more often than not he would.

20

Big In New York

BOBBY stood alone in front of 56,000 Cosmos fans in Giants Stadium, New Jersey, who all wanted him to fail. It was August 1980 and he hadn't scored all season. This wouldn't have been such a big deal in England, as August is the month the football season begins, but the lack of goals to your name is not so good for confidence when you're an attacking player during a summer season that starts in April. If the lack of goals hadn't been bad enough for his confidence, the over-riding reason for that statistic made more depressing reading: more often than not he was out of the starting Washington Diplomats line-up during the 1980 season.

But here was an opportunity for some glory. The Dips had drawn 1-1 with the Cosmos after 90 minutes so it was time for another shoot-out. Bobby had the ball at his feet on the 35-yard line. Once the referee blew the whistle he had five seconds to score, but things didn't bode well for the Dips. Two things tended to happen when they played the Cosmos; the game would go to a deciding shoot-out and the Dips would lose. Or at least this is what had happened the last three times the two had faced each other. Scoring four goals at Giants Stadium the previous season wasn't enough for the Dips, who after sharing a 4-4 draw ended up losing in yet another shoot-out.

History was clearly on the Cosmos' side. So was recent form. They went in having won their previous 14 consecutive home games. On the upside, the Dips had plenty of recent shoot-out practice. Not that it had done them much good as they'd missed their last 12 shoot-out attempts. The writing was very much on the wall. Frankly, when it came to shoot-outs, the Dips stank and they knew it.

They'd had to fight back to even make the shoot-out, levelling the game only 25 seconds after going a goal down. Bobby was in on the action, but had to be patient, being brought on as substitute with around half an hour left and was later named fifth in line to take a kick in the shoot-out. More often than not this was the pressure kick. The Dips had scored their first three attempts, but Johan Cruyff, the star player of team and the entire league, had missed their fourth. If Bobby scored the Dips would beat the Cosmos. And he did, sending a right-footer beneath goalkeeper Hubert Birkenmeier. It was the biggest win in the franchise's seven-year history. Other than the FA Cup Final it was a moment of glory every bit as big as Bobby had experienced before.

The *New York Times* was cool on the subject. It was keen to put the result in context – the Cosmos were without Franz Beckenbauer and Johan Neeskens, which loosely translated to, 'Had these two played then the Cosmos would have wiped the floor with Washington.' Some of the Cosmos' playing roster were less than impressed with how the Dips went about their business. Ricky Davis, perhaps not used to losing, sounded a little sour. 'It wasn't enough for them to come here and play well,' he said. 'They had to bicker and complain and shout. It wasn't necessary for them to play with their mouths.'

Bobby could have been forgiven for getting carried away in the heat of the moment, but he took it all in his stride. 'Don't call me a hero,' he shouted at team-mates as he was interviewed after the game. He was one of the few to volunteer to be involved in the shoot-out. Dips coach Gordon Bradley had faith in him, despite his scoreless run during the 1980 season. 'When I looked on my line-up card I said, "Oh, here's Bobby." He looked at me and said, "No problem. I'll go." He's a sure-footed player and I had confidence he would make it.'

Bobby was also confident. 'I've always had pretty good luck in the shoot-outs, so I didn't feel nervous about taking that last kick,' he said. But as ever he remained humble, ensuring his team-mates were given equal billing when it came to dishing out the plaudits, 'Remember, I wasn't the only player who made kicks. Fortunately, when they [Cosmos] missed it took a lot of pressure off me. It felt nice to come up to New York and do something special, especially against these guys.' Pelé may have long gone, but the Cosmos still had plenty of talent to call on, including Brazil's World Cup-winning captain Carlos Alberto and the NASL's all-time leading goalscorer and all-round pantomime villain Giorgio Chinaglia, who had put the Cosmos ahead from the penalty spot with seven minutes remaining.

The post-match reaction from some of Bobby's team-mates clearly demonstrated that the Dips had got a serious monkey off of their backs by beating the Cosmos. The reactions ranged from righteous, when Canadian midfielder Carmine Marcantonio said, 'God finally did justice,' to sheer relief from Alan Green, 'At last we won one of these bloody things.' Of course, the Dips had beaten the Cosmos before. But the 2-1 win in 1977 was a dead rubber. The stakes were much higher this time around. It was in the Cosmos' backyard, where the Dips had endured some pretty terrible results in the past. The win also clinched their place in the play-offs and with it a shot at the Soccer Bowl, which was due to be played on the home turf of RFK in Washington.

Given the context of the result, opposition and setting it stands to reason that this game would have generated some pretty strong memories. But, 36 years down the line, nobody seems to remember that game. Dave Wasser, from Austin, Texas, has an extensive selection of games from the North American Soccer League between 1975 and 1983 available to order on DVD. You can watch Rochester Lancers pinch a 1-0 win at Portland in front of 8,000 fans, or enjoy seeing Tulsa Roughnecks socking it 3-1 against Edmonton Drillers, but you try finding footage of the Dips' win against Cosmos in 1980. It doesn't exist. Maybe Giorgio Chinaglia and the Cosmos' public relations department had the tapes burnt to cinders?

The lack of recall stretches to Bobby's team-mates. By 1980, Jim Steele and Paul Cannell had moved on. Ray Graydon can remember the President's Cup, but he only had a season at RFK – he'd moved on by 1980. Eric Martin had retired due to injury; Bill Irwin likewise. The quotes from Alan Green and Carmine Marcantonio were from the time. Ask them now and they stop and think. So does Tommy O'Hara. They all remember the home game with the Cosmos in June 1980. A 50,000-plus crowd showed up for that one too. It was a huge crowd to have at RFK for a soccer game but the Dips lost, again on a shoot-out. They lost quite spectacularly, failing to score any of their shoot-out attempts.

Bobby didn't even play in that game. So why do his team-mates remember losing to but not beating the Cosmos? Had their old adversaries had such a huge effect they had burnt failure on to their collective consciousness? Maybe, but the huge home crowd and televised nature of the game probably has more to do with it. Bobby would have probably remembered that game too, but not for good reasons. Carmine Marcantonio recalls Bobby being a bit fed up at this stage. 'He took it like a good professional,' he said. 'But his role in the starting XI diminished when Johan Cruyff joined us. We tended to play with one striker, with a number-ten-type of player just off him.' Bobby was a good player, but Johan Cruyff was one of the greatest ever. There was no dice there – Cruyff would play in that free role. Cruyff could be outspoken and critical of team-mates, as well as often being right. His Dutch international team-mate Willem van Hanegem was having problems with a hotel vending machine spitting out his coins, when Cruyff advised him to insert the coins using a short, dry throw, which of course worked, but which also wound van Hanegem up no end.

Three years earlier Bobby had named Cruyff as his favourite player in the club yearbook. Now the Dutchman was squeezing Bobby out of the side, as well as having considerable influence over the team. Naturally, as the player synonymous with the term total football, he wasn't keen on any direct style of play, preferring a build-up on the floor while playing to more of a diamond formation.

Johan was one of the guys, up to a certain point. 'He'd put the team first,' said Carmine. 'And you couldn't shut him up on the pitch – he was always communicating, orchestrating, helping you to make the right decision with the ball. He was always available to receive the ball as well – it was like he was three steps ahead.' Total football doesn't mean passing and prettiness for the sake of passing, because as Carmine says, 'Johan hated losing.' He still had it too, scoring a memorable goal against Seattle Sounders, when he ran from the halfway line in a series of shimmies and sprints. Bobby was in awe, telling newspapers, 'That was the goal of the season – Johan was on that ball like a puma, it was like he was saying catch me if you can.'

Cruyff was later interviewed wearing an ice pack on a heavily bandaged thigh as he smoked a cigarette, telling reporters, 'The only person allowed to lose the ball is me, because when I do there are seven players behind me.' Some may have put him in the diva category, but if anyone had the talent to truly merit that status it was Johan Cruyff.

Bobby wasn't prone to sulking about his limited first-team opportunities. 'Bobby was one of the guys who'd make life happy on a long journey – we'd play bullshit poker and seven card stud the night before a game,' said Carmine. To his Canadian-Italian ears, Bobby and Mike Dillon sounded like extras from the cast of *Mary Poppins*.

The 1980 season was Bobby's last shot at glory with the Dips. It wasn't to be. Bobby combined with Cruyff to score the only goal of the game in the home leg of the play-off game with Los Angeles Aztecs, drawing praise from Cruyff, who said, 'It was a good goal. He made a good shot, I just gave him the pass.' Perhaps not gushing in his admiration, but Cruyff wasn't one to fall over people when it came to praise, so this was a significant tip of the hat to Bobby.

But the Dips lost out in the second leg. Their old nemesis, New York Cosmos, won the Soccer Bowl that season and the Dips were finished. Average home attendances had grown year on year but they were falling a little short of the average 20,000 home crowds the franchise owners needed to break even, so they pulled their investment. The Dips would be given a new lease of life but it wasn't the same. Jimmy Hill was calling the shots in his role as the new franchise owner. The Dips side that people knew and loved had gone and Bobby's professional career was over at the age of 29.

21

Constant Question

NEWS of Bobby's glory with the Diplomats in New York did not travel well. The *Washington Post* is not widely read in Chichester, who Bobby began playing for in 1981, just a year after his shoot-out glory against the Cosmos. No one would blame him for clinging on to the memory of that game, perhaps pointing to the soles of his feet and explaining that the clods of grass hugging his studded soles was from the turf of Giants Stadium, New Jersey. Had he done so, it's unlikely anyone would have pointed out that the only grass around Giants Stadium was a few blocks away from the vast parking lot surrounding Meadowlands Sports Complex. This is because the turf there was artificial. But it was never a talking point – football in the USA was a different and distant world. And if Bobby was so good what was he doing playing in the Sussex County League?

Bobby was no self-publicist though. He would never have brought it up unless asked and that was unlikely. For those plying their trade in the Sussex County League, discussing how you got one over Brazil's World Cup-winning captain Carlos Alberto in Giants Stadium wasn't likely to crop up in conversation. If Bobby had decided to add in the fact he'd done the business where his team-mate Johan Cruyff had failed, those listening would dismiss him as a fantasist, or worse still, a name-dropper and a bragger. Despite the glory, Bobby was well aware of the wider context of his final summer season spent in the States. This high-water mark had been towards the end of an otherwise disappointing season for him personally. Bobby was competing against Johan Cruyff to get in the side. Everyone played second fiddle to Cruyff and Bobby was no different. Even if the Dutchman didn't perform, he would always play. He was the franchise's marquee player more than 30 years before the phrase had become common in British football.

Once Washington lost the franchise Bobby was home again. Everything was different back in England but it would remain the same forever. His career as a professional footballer was over a good five months shy of his 30th birthday. There was no getting away from hanging up your boots – it was inevitable, you couldn't play forever, but all too many players from Bobby's era were far better equipped to face up to the tough challenges on the field, like being knocked into next week by the likes of Billy Bremner and Tommy Smith, than working out what exactly they would do with their lives once they could no longer earn a living from playing football.

Perhaps the biggest factor is not what they were leaving behind, but what they were faced with. Potentially it meant resigning themselves to a life that may never derive the same pleasure and satisfaction provided by playing the game they loved. Bobby wasn't hanging up his boots entirely though, as Chichester City still provided him with a much needed outlet. Bobby made his Chichester debut at Southwick on 19 August 1981 – a year and a day after his winning shoot-out attempt in New York. The signing was low key, so much so that club chairman Trevor Wallis only found out about it on the night of his debut, 'Richie Reynolds showed me the teamsheet and I saw the name Bobby Stokes in the starting XI – I asked him if it was *the* Bobby Stokes and he just told me in a very matter of fact way that Bobby had agreed to play a few games for us.' Trevor ended up being Bobby's chaperone to games around the county.

When a non-league club signs a former professional one of the first questions the chairman tends to ask is, 'How much are we paying him?' But Trevor doesn't remember Bobby being paid anything to play. 'I used to pick him up on Saturday afternoon. If my wife was with me, Bobby would sit in the back seat with my dog. I found Bobby a very modest and unassuming lad.'

Greg Brown was a young man and club captain when Bobby arrived alongside him in Chichester City's midfield. 'I was in awe of him,' said Greg. 'Bobby trained and played like one of the regular lads. Not like all ex-pros, who might have airs and graces about them and might not fancy it in non-league and be a bit aloof. Bobby wasn't like that.' Chichester's manager Richie Reynolds had been Portsmouth's Player of the Year less than a decade earlier. He had arrived at the club in a puff of smoke and a Ford Capri while Chichester were struggling at the bottom of the county league table in early 1979. The following season they were champions. They have only achieved that once since, although not in Bobby's time. 'Bobby was an unimposing figure who got on with it,' added Greg. 'He had that bit of class – he knew where to go and when and didn't need to expend energy if it wasn't required.' Greg appreciated that although Bobby was an ex-professional he couldn't simply waltz past the opposition. 'He wasn't a game-changer, but his first touch and good command of the basic skills gave him more time on the ball than everyone else.'

Opposition players would hone in on Bobby in the bar after games. 'He was asked endlessly about his cup final goal,' said Trevor. 'Invariably he said the same thing when quizzed whether he was offside, along the lines of, "The referee and linesman didn't think so – check the record books." Any misgivings of first meeting Bobby were soon waylaid after a few pints. It was as though he was being forever challenged about the goal, mainly by Pompey fans. Spending so much time with him I got tired of this question – I found it quite rude, but Bobby never did – he was very mild-mannered off the field.' But Maria Johnson remembers Bobby being firm on the subject if he was sufficiently provoked. 'He wouldn't be nasty, but if people went on about him being offside he would say to them, "But I scored that goal, what have you done?"'

The 1982/83 season was a poor one for Chichester, which saw them lose 27 of 28 games between September and March. Reynolds had left and the subsequent manager was sacked during this period. 'Bobby was one of only about two players who stayed loyal to the club,' said Trevor. The others left for rival clubs in the continual merry-go-round of non-league football.

Trevor spent much of this time worrying himself sick about the club being relegated. It didn't seem to concern Bobby at all. To Trevor, Bobby showed no signs of frustration about the lesser squad that now surrounded him or their dire form. It wasn't that he didn't care, he just seemed content playing.

The car journeys around the Sussex countryside to Rye, Bexhill and Hastings gave Bobby ample opportunity to walk down memory lane as well as provide the chance to polish his after-dinner speaking act – which was the potential avenue for retired footballers to earn some money and enjoy a few beers – and spin a few yarns about the scrapes he and Ossie had got into.

But Trevor doesn't ever recall him saying anything of the sort. 'Bobby wasn't the type of lad to tell anecdotes about his playing career. He was never interested in where we were going either, he just seemed glad to be off out on a Saturday afternoon for a kick-about.' As a result, news of Bobby's USA glory in New York came as a further surprise to Trevor, who said, 'He never mentioned it.'

The only bright spot on the field during this spell was a 3-1 cup win in November at Hailsham, a town in East Sussex, situated further inland than Chichester, just off the A22. With no coast to boast of the town took its chances with convenience over beauty, making do with its pedestrianised high street. The weather had been miserable. When the rain stopped the club volunteers assessed the damage to the Hailsham pitch. With Chichester's form suggesting they were sitting ducks they did everything they could to get the game on. It backfired, with a rare glimpse of Chichester's potential in an otherwise poor season. The heavy rain tested the commitment of local fans. Not that the game went ahead in front of the proverbial one man and his dog. 'There were maybe 100 there at most,' said Greg. 'They had a corner, but we broke away towards their end. I played a ball wide to the right while Bobby was making a great run towards the back post. The cross found him and he rose Martin Peters-like from the inside-left channel to head the ball over the keeper, sending the ball back where it came from.'

It wasn't just the goal that sticks in Greg's mind, but Bobby's broad grin, too. It remained as they high-fived and returned to the centre circle for the restart. Forget the weather, forget the location: Wembley, New York, Hailsham – it didn't matter. A goal was a goal and Bobby would enjoy it, albeit relatively quietly.

There were other goals to remember at Chichester. The Coronation Cup was an annual pre-season game with Petersfield. 'We'd dropped off in standard by this time,' admits Greg. 'We were three down at half-time.' Then right after the break Bobby reminded everyone of what a clean striker of the ball he could be. 'The ball came down from some height and he walloped it past the keeper – it was a great strike,' said Greg. Sadly, it was past his own goalkeeper. 'It was one of the most remarkable own goals I've ever seen,' said Trevor. 'Bobby thrashed a piledriver past our own keeper from something like the halfway line. It was as though he had forgotten we'd changed ends,' added Greg. 'Nobody said anything, not even Bobby – he just seemed to block it out.'

Trevor later sought an explanation on the drive home. 'I asked him afterwards why he did that. His reply was, "I forgot we changed ends at half-time." I never really found out the truth.' Trevor's dog did what he could to save face for Bobby by trying to cause an equally memorable incident, managing to hold the game up by running on to the field with a recently caught shrew in his jaws. He was chased by Trevor, but the shrew escaped, the dog was annoyed and Trevor got a good telling-off from the referee.

As the 1980s drew on Bobby's reputation was no longer sufficient to hold down a starting place in the Chichester City starting XI. Younger men were coming through the ranks and, as Brian O'Neil said, you need young legs.

Bobby appeared in around half of Chichester's games in the 1983/84 season but was reduced to a handful of games in the season that followed. At 33 his fitness was on the wane and he was starting to show the signs of a drinker's paunch. Not that Bobby was overweight, if anything he was the opposite, but the chiselled and slim physique gained by daily training had vanished – perhaps not helped by the fact Bobby wasn't required to train with the club.

Trevor was a diligent keeper of club records: Bobby made 87 starts for Chichester City, with six further appearances as a substitute. In that time he scored eight goals. His spell at the club ended at the age of 34 with a substitute appearance against East Grinstead. The football wasn't enough though, Bobby needed work now. This wasn't unusual – in fact it was par for the course for all footballers of that era. The vast majority of Bobby's peers wouldn't have earned anyway near enough to see out their days playing golf. As Lawrie McMenemy said, none of his players could put their feet up, they all had to get jobs after football, even Kevin Keegan.

Not that former professional footballers' loss of direction is purely down to a lack of money. There have been many cases in recent years of players suffering from depression once their careers have finished. Then there are those who have lost their money. Former England goalkeeper David James is a good example. Supposedly intelligent and handsomely well paid over the course of a career spanning 20 years, he was declared bankrupt in 2014. It would be foolish to believe James will be the last highly-paid player to suffer the same fate.

Admittedly, for those who have played in the Premier League there are more career options than there were in Bobby's day: get a new haircut and a designer suit, become a pundit on the TV or the radio, write a syndicated newspaper column, build an audience through a social media profile and stand for election, even wear a dress, change your name to Rita and get caught with your trousers down with a local MP in the windows of Harrods – it doesn't matter, there's always a career angle. Sell your story to the tabloids; if someone's beaten you to it, do the reality TV circuit – show the world what you've got, for good or ill. That world didn't exist when Bobby's professional career ended in 1980 and frankly, he'd have run a country mile from it. He never went looking for the spotlight. But he didn't need to, it always came looking for him.

The career path of the ex-footballer in the 1980s was clearly defined, albeit with narrow horizons. 'Bobby spent his life off the field searching for the sense of belonging that he found as a player. When Bobby's football finished, part of him finished, too. He missed the lads dreadfully.' These are the words of Bobby's wife Janet at the time of his death. Belonging is very much the operative word: that's what football gave Bobby. It also gave him structure and purpose. Take those things away from a man and he can find himself cut adrift very quickly.

That lack of structure can be a problem, as Ray Graydon explains, 'I never had an operation as a player, but I'm making up for it now – my back's playing up. An operation might stop me from playing golf, but it won't cause me to self-destruct though.' Ray paused. 'I don't know about Bobby though. I'm already thinking about the next thing in my life – go away with my wife, spend time with the grandkids, go for a walk – I can still get out and about. Bob couldn't do that. He'd be phoning Ossie, asking when they can meet up.'

Football was everything to Bobby. It was also everything to Ray, but he was able to find other things in his life to occupy himself with. Many former Southampton players found work down the docks. Irishman Tommy Traynor played more than 400 games for the club in the 1950s and 60s before working down the docks, the same post-football employment as Bobby McLaughlin and Denis Hollywood, who was available on a free transfer and left Southampton in 1972. The passing years have smoothed out any bitterness, not that Denis is that way inclined.

He had options – Blackpool were in for him. 'Ted Bates told me that if I was sensible I'd make a lot of money,' said Denis. 'Well, I didn't.' He went to Blackpool, but it didn't work out. Before long he had returned to Southampton to work up on the container berth for Union Castle. The transition was tricky at the time. 'It took me a couple of years to adjust to giving up,' said Denis. 'It was the laughing and joking you missed.'

Luck plays its part. You get your breaks, but as Bob McCarthy says, 'Some players can't release themselves from the game – giving up hits you hard.' Bob went on to play in the Southern League but the experience of being released from Southampton, his home-town team, left him somewhat disillusioned with the game. He got a job working in sales for Coca-Cola – he didn't want to scratch around playing in the lower leagues as a professional. 'It took a few years to get it out of my system,' said Bob. 'It's your life. You've got to get on with it and put any unhappy memories of being released behind you.' While maintaining an interest in Southampton's fortunes, neither Bob nor Denis watch the game religiously today. 'A lot of players don't make good spectators,' said Bob. 'They want to play the game, not watch it. You get frustrated watching it.'

Being an ex-player isn't enough on its own to get you work but you've still got to earn a living. Brian O'Neil is pretty straightforward on the subject of life after football. He worked labouring for Trants for 12 years. 'A bit of hard work never killed anyone. I had run some miles in my life since starting as a footballer at 15, but by the time I packed in I had two kids to support – you've got to get on with it,' said Brian, who retired from playing at 34. He enjoyed the physical work as much as he did quenching his thirst in the pub by the time he'd worked for six days a week. Hugh Fisher went into sales and marketing for Foster's, which he described as a great job, with plenty of golf days. Mick Judd and Paul Gilchrist had the rug pulled from beneath their feet when injuries forced them into early retirement from the game, but both rebuilt their lives with good careers. Mick Channon is still thriving in his second career as a racehorse trainer. This was a lifelong passion, something he worked hard on throughout his football career, but Mick plays it down. 'I've been fortunate,' he said. 'Packing up football was one of the hardest things in our day.' What to do? Many players ended up running a pub. And why not? The drinks, the camaraderie; the good times back as quick as it takes to have a drink or two. Channon's eyes widen on the subject of becoming a publican, 'That could be the road to ruin.'

Many former players became landlords. Some of them were perhaps better suited to life on the other side of the bar, where they could be the larger-than-life character the role required. Jimmy McGowan was a successful publican. McGowan started his footballing career in the Celtic youth team, but the Scot spent the majority of the 1950s playing as an attacker for Southampton. Like so many of the club's former players he remained in the area, becoming landlord of the Drummond Arms in Portswood, a suburb a few miles outside of the city centre. The pub has a special place in the club's folklore. Jim Steele lodged there for a time while a Southampton player. Jim, along with Bobby and Peter Osgood, pinched the FA Cup and took it to the pub. The locals drank from it, before they took it into town and then on to a burger bar. The trophy was eventually returned to The Dell. It was a nice little story for Jimmy McGowan to trade in on – that the FA Cup was on his premises only a few days after the big game.

It wasn't always like this. Not every day is a party. In 1984, McGowan was found by schoolchildren in the boating lake at Southampton Common. Paramedics fished his body out of the water with a canoe amid rumours of debts and suicide. Jimmy's death shone a light on the difficulties footballers had in adjusting to life after their playing careers had finished.

This is where life took Bobby as he became landlord of the Manor House in Cosham. It was left to Nick Holmes to highlight the initial sense of isolation that can sweep over you the day you have to hang up your boots. 'After our football careers we'd all meet up from time to time. Bobby seemed to come to life during those times. We're in our 60s and 70s now, but when the lads meet up there's still that buzz, and you miss it. I mean, flipping heck, I still go to bed dreaming about football. It's still there and I don't give a monkey's what anyone says, when you're a young man playing football they are the best days of your life.'

22

Lord Of The Manor

'THE only time I ever remember Bobby getting called a Scummer was one New Year's Eve,' said Gordon Smith, who was a local at the Manor House, where Bobby was landlord during the 1980s. 'He disappeared upstairs then came down in his red and white Southampton shirt from the Charity Shield at Wembley. He was stood behind the bar and the whole pub went, "Scummer, Scummer, Scummer".' Binge drinking stirred up tribal feelings when presented with the sight of red and white stripes, but on this occasion the chants were born out of reflex rather than malice. In Gordon's experience drinking at the pub it was a rare occurrence of Bobby's Southampton connections being used as a stick to beat him with.

Gordon, along with brothers Chris and Kevin Sibley, and Gary Edwards, were all die-hard Portsmouth fans and recent school leavers when they started drinking in the Manor House in 1983. Close to Paulsgrove, the pub can be found off the Cosham high street, among residential housing. The building is more in keeping with a small school than a pub – red-bricked and tiled and very wide inside, the bar alone is longer than the width of two penalty areas. A picture in one far corner of the pub looks like a shot of a Greek fishing village, when it is in actual fact the nearby Portsmouth water on a sunny day. Photoshop has a lot to answer for.

'Bobby had a sharp sense of humour,' said Gary. 'I remember someone pointing at him saying, "That man scored a goal at Wembley," and Bobby turned around and said, "No I didn't, I was offside." It was one of his regular lines. There was never any animosity towards him. He was well known in Paulsgrove, so he was respected – he was a down-to-earth working-class bloke. No one had anything bad to say about him.'

'Yeah, if people asked him I'm sure he'd talk about the cup final,' added Chris. 'But I can't remember him ever saying anything about it or his football career – he was very quiet about it.' There were no trinkets from the past used to decorate the pub either, 'I don't remember him having a single picture of his playing days on the wall either,' added Kevin.

The four would come to know Bobby as well as young locals can hope to know their local's landlord, although the relationship appeared to be short-lived at first. 'The first time we came in we all got thrown out,' said Gordon. 'About ten of us had walked down from the Salisbury,' another now-disappeared pub that then had a penchant for serving the underage regardless of how slapdash their fake ID was. But Gordon and his friends had their eyes on the Manor House because it had something the Salisbury didn't – a pool table. 'We managed to get served – not by Bobby though,' said Gordon. 'We took our drinks round the corner, then Bobby walked up to us all and says, "Right, I don't think any of you are overage – so drink up and leave." So we did.'

Gordon remained persistent, becoming a regular face at the pub, 'I used to keep coming, using my fake ID, I'd been drinking there a while before I turned 18.' During this time Gordon started the pub pool team, which he captained, bringing the lads into his seven-man group. It all helped him to become a local while also proving himself to be a shrewd economist, using the dead time between two and five in the afternoon when pubs closed to hone his technique with free games by stuffing the pool table's pockets with beer towels from the bar.

When Gordon did become legally old enough to drink he decided to mark the occasion at the Manor House. 'It was a Thursday night and I wasn't doing anything special so I went to the pub,' he said. 'Word got round at the bar it was my birthday. Bobby came up to me and says, "I've been told it's your birthday, Gordon – how old are you?" I said, "Sorry Bobby, I'm 18." From behind his back he produced this huge glass of brandy and said, get that down you.' Bobby had a good heart. It helped him get away with wearing a Southampton shirt in a Portsmouth pub. Could anyone else do the same?

'You'd be all right,' said Gary. 'It'd be cowardice ganging up on one bloke.'

'There's a time and place though,' added Chris. 'We played local football for 30 years and in all that time I never saw a team play in red and white stripes. You imagine the football catalogues come around at the start of the season and everyone's like, yeah, we'll get the Brazil kit, we'll get a green one, or a blue one, but down here you might as well cross the page out that has red and white stripes.'

Gary highlighted a local derby played on a Sunday morning a few years back, 'They moved all the Sunday league games to the afternoon and a friend of mine was playing at the King George playing fields in Cosham when a train full of Southampton fans stopped at signals next to the pitches. He reckons every single player from every game, including referees, stopped to run and shout "Scummer" at the train.

'That's the sort of mentality,' said Gary. 'Then there's another lad we know – he used to be a 6:57-er,' which refers to the 6:57 Crew, Portsmouth's hooligan firm from the 1980s, named after the time they caught the early morning train en route to games in London. 'He was at a music festival in Southsea – he's grown up now, he's a 50-year-old man, but he's got Pompey tattoos all over his legs; anyway, he went to get a drink and he came back and he couldn't speak. He'd been talking to this bloke about what a great day it was and that we'd gone 1-0 up and the bloke had said, "What team's that?" When he said Pompey, the other bloke said, "My team's losing." What team? "Saints!" He didn't know whether to hit him or speak, that this bloke had the front to say that.'

The two sets of fans do mix more often than people tend to realise. 'Last week we were playing five-a-side in Fareham in our Pompey tops and there was a bloke with a Southampton tattoo walking past,' said Kevin, who spent ten years working for Vosper Thorneycroft, a shipbuilding firm based in Woolston in Southampton, where the alliance of apprentices would be split down the middle. 'So much animosity at games but you're sitting next to them at work,' said Kevin.

His brother Chris has had similar experiences, finding himself recently getting pulled up by the security guard at his work. 'He's Pompey through and through,' said Chris. 'I had a red and white checked shirt on that day and he wanted to know why I was wearing it. I was like, what are you talking about?' Chris works in Whiteley, just off junction nine of the M27. 'That's the divide,' added Chris. 'You see the occasional red and white shirt and a few blue ones.'

It's a divide, but a sedate one too. Nearby Locks Heath is home to a large Waitrose. It never kicks off in Waitrose, not unless they run out of ginseng powder or organic humus, but never because of something as crass as an alliance to a sports team. There was rarely any trouble at the Manor House either. It wasn't that kind of pub. When they all started drinking there in 1983 Bobby was only 32, which came as something of a surprise to the group when discussing it more than 30 years later. 'Was he?' asked Kevin. 'Thirty-two? He should have still been playing.'

'It was only seven years after the cup final,' said Chris. 'It's the equivalent of Kanu running the pub now – he'd be treated like an absolute legend.' Kanu scored Portsmouth's winning goal in the 2008 FA Cup Final.

Bobby was still playing during his days at the Manor House, although making up the back four with Gary Edwards at a local all-weather pitch down the road probably doesn't constitute still playing. 'Playing a few games with Bobby was brilliant,' recalled Gary. 'He played centre-back with me and I probably had the best game of my life.'

'And this from a man who doesn't play football,' laughed Chris.

'Yeah,' agreed Kevin. 'That was on the Astroturf down the Mountbatten Centre against Hendy Fords.' Gary believes his own good form was down to Bobby, who coached him through the game, telling him when to step up from defence.

'Maybe our perception was he was an average player,' said Kevin. 'But when we played with him, well…'

'He just strolled around, hardly moving,' added Gary. 'But he read the game so well you could tell he was a professional. He once told me he wasn't that happy in the job, that it wasn't quite right for him. The responsibility fell on him heavily – maybe he was too nice.'

Kevin could sympathise, 'Seven days a week – working as an old-school pub landlord you got no time off.'

'It'd be a bit like being stuck in a sweet shop,' added Gary. 'But I never saw him pissed.' They remember him on both sides of the bar, his tipple was a brandy and coke. By the time the four lads hit their 20s they were going further afield than the Manor House for a night out and although news of Bobby leaving the pub wasn't a huge surprise, the exact reason for him doing so was not known to them.

Old schoolfriend Steve Hatton compares Bobby's position in Portsmouth in the same way you might admire or respect a politician who might represent a party you don't vote for. It's certainly unusual, but it does very occasionally happen. Despite the inter-city rivalry people could see beyond it. Real life wasn't a cartoon. 'Bob was someone who just chatted,' said Steve, who grew up with Bobby in Paulsgrove. 'I bumped into him several times later on after his career and he would always stop and chat.'

Steve recalls one occasion at Kimbells, a venue in Portsmouth which was being used for a dinner and dance. Bobby's wife had a dance school for youngsters and they had been invited along to provide a small cabaret event during the evening. 'Bob was just back from the US and was telling me all about his experiences there,' said Steve. 'The razzmatazz, coming out on to the pitch on Harleys and that kind of thing; he kept telling me it should have been me there'. Steve thought that was an unusual thing to say. Although it was only a brief conversation it has always stuck in Steve's mind. 'It was as if he really felt I was somehow more deserving of his footballing experiences in America than he was, which I really don't understand,' said Steve. 'Whether Bobby felt because I was a teacher I was somehow more deserving, I really don't know, but I think that says a lot about his thought process – in Bobby's mind, he was just Bob from around the corner and he seemed almost embarrassed by the acclaim he received for his success as a footballer.'

Ray Graydon called in on Bobby at the Manor House on his way to Fratton Park as a scout for Oxford United. It was lunchtime and Ray saw Bobby sat on a stool at the bar in an empty pub. He looked so small to Ray in the pub's cavernous interior. 'He looked tiny sat there,' said Ray. 'And he sounded lonely and lost – that wasn't the Bobby I knew. I left feeling very sad for him.'

Maria Johnson didn't think Bobby was business-minded enough to run a pub. 'The job got hold of him,' said Maria. 'With everyone going to the pub and when they went to pay he would say, "No, no, no – you have that on me." When you're in business you can't do that.' Things went downhill. Maria questioned Bobby's methods. She used to work nearby and often popped into the pub at lunchtime, where Bobby would refuse to take his cousin's money. Maria would shake her head and told Bobby's wife she'd have to put a stop to it all. She told Maria that they'd have to get out of the pub game because they weren't making any money. Bobby was just too nice to be a pub landlord.

23

Menial

BY the mid-1980s Bobby was no longer a pub landlord. His old friend Peter Osgood ran a soccer school, getting Bobby involved in coaching sessions for budding footballers whose parents were more interested in the former Southampton man than their children. They were too young to have seen Bobby play. Their Saints heroes were Mark Dennis and Danny Wallace, younger men with more angular haircuts than the slight individual stood before them watching them dribble in and out of a line of cones. It didn't quite register when their dads told them about Bobby's famous goal. While they couldn't articulate it, they felt Bobby didn't carry himself in the manner expected of someone whose goal was responsible for winning the FA Cup. Where was the strut, the swagger, and all the other unspoken body language traits of someone who had done what they could only fantasise about? They didn't exist.

The work wasn't enough for Bobby to earn a living. John Robson looked to have the answer. As the owner of a heating and plumbing business, John had done work for many former Southampton players, including Bobby. This work earned him an occasional starting place alongside Bobby in Southampton's old boys' team. Not that John's inclusion in such esteemed company was a magnanimous gesture based solely on his thorough work de-scaling radiators. John was a former professional footballer in Scotland so was a more than adequate recruit if the team needed an extra body. Word got around John needed an extra pair of hands. Bobby couldn't bring himself to broach the subject with John, who was eventually called on the subject by Bobby's dad. He told John that his son would never ask for anything or look for responsibility. Calling about work would have been excruciating for him.

Responsibility was something he would only take upon himself in the confines of a football match, when in possession of the ball and with thousands of pairs of eyes upon him. The contradiction was obvious. Football was Bobby's comfort zone, everything else existed outside of it, and as such, was a world he was far less comfortable operating in. John was happy to take 'Stokesy' on as his labourer. Although not the first footballer to go on to do a spot of menial work, Bobby was perhaps the only one to join his boss for a game of crossbar challenge during lunchtime. 'We used to keep a ball in the back of the van,' said John, who along with Bobby would hone in on the whites of a set of posts. 'It all started after we did a job for Chichester City. We'd be aiming for the post or crossbar from outside the D of the penalty area; Bobby would absolutely murder me – he'd be hitting the bar a good four times out of five.'

John and Bobby's work together constituted more than a lunchtime kick-about. They soon became good friends. 'We'd never fall out. I gave him plenty of stick, sometimes. He never gave it back, sometimes I wish he did. Now and then I'd get a call in the morning from his wife, telling me

Bobby wasn't coming into work.' John wouldn't be angry though. 'There was something about him,' added John. 'Even if he did let you down you couldn't help but like him.'

A lunchtime knock could never compensate for the real thing. Football never went away. You didn't have to see it to feel its absence. If the wind blew in the right direction then it came calling on the breeze from the nearest local football pitch. Terse instructions like 'man on' and 'time' killed the relative quiet of a Saturday afternoon or a Sunday morning, interrupted by higher-pitched pleads of 'ref' and shrill blasts of a whistle.

The senses could overwhelm you. The unstinting optimism that comes from the smell of freshly-cut grass could trigger the brain to assume a position on the back post for an incoming cross from Terry Paine. The memories of Bobby's career remained intact, but reliving them wasn't much use. The real thrill in scoring a goal came in the very moment of doing so. Trying to piece it back together in your mind during the quiet of a Tuesday afternoon was like trying to make a rainbow out of clay. When you did have the time and space to play the memories back in your mind it only served as a reminder of how much time has passed since. It was a downer. Better to leave the memories to play gently in the back seat of your mind, where they could be preserved.

Any former Southampton players in need of scratching the itch that came from having hung up their boots could find temporary relief turning out for the ex-Saints side. Roy Beazley was heavily involved in the Ex-Saints Association. If Southampton Football Club ever decide to open a museum they'd do well to get in touch with Roy. A room in his house is dedicated to Southampton memorabilia. On first inspection it's too much to take in – too many goodies to identify all at once. An England cap which originally belonged to Mick Channon for a game against Czechoslovakia in 1974 sticks out, as does Channon's Admiral, Don Revie-era England jersey, complete with grass stains.

Equally impressive is Roy's address book. Kept on a shelf alongside his armchair, next to a packet of biscuits that had been neatly rolled up in order to protect them from going stale, Roy's book catalogues the great and the good at Southampton over the years, their names and numbers written neatly in black capitals. Roy knew Bobby for 25 years during his involvement with the Ex-Saints Association. He would organise between eight and ten games a year for former players. Nobody would be paid, but the money raised in ticket sales would be donated to local charities. Roy was involved with the association for 45 years. During that time the association raised £4m, resulting in him being awarded an MBE which hangs on the wall of his lounge.

'Bobby would do anything for you,' said Roy. 'At the same time he relied on other people too. He seemed to come to life at ex-Saints games. He loved it.' Denis Hollywood would be one of many players involved. No longer in the shape he was in during his playing days and having vowed to never get involved with anything to do with such matches, here he was, with most of his old pals. The lure of the dressing room and a few post-match beers was all it took.

Games would normally be played at modest, local grounds. But on one occasion they were invited to play a Brentford side at Wembley in the early 1990s. It was a big deal for Roy. 'A few days before the game Bobby rang me up,' said Roy. 'He told me I ought to play at Wembley – he was quite insistent about it.' Roy wondered what Bobby was going on about. Although Roy had played as a striker at a decent level as a younger man, by then he was in his 50s. Although the games weren't life and death, they weren't a complete joke either. He wasn't motivated by using his clout as some kind of leverage to blag a game at Wembley, but Bobby wouldn't leave it alone. The team travelled up to Wembley in a minibus. 'There were all these posh coaches going past us on the journey up the M3 and we're in this minibus with all the lads,' said Roy. 'We parked up at Wembley and headed for the changing rooms and Bobby was at it again, telling me I'm playing. So in the end I did – I was a bag of nerves.'

Bobby's advice for Roy was simple, 'He told me to just go and enjoy myself. He seemed to think I deserved to play. I ended up playing the whole 90 minutes in the middle of the park alongside Jimmy Case.' Everything people said about the size of the Wembley pitch seemed true to Roy. The wings seemed to slope away into the distance. 'Whenever I got the ball I just looked to play short passes in to Jimmy.' The last thing Roy wanted to do was let anybody down. The knock-on effect being he didn't really want the ball, playing in a conservative, holding midfield style of play. As the match wore on Jimmy began to twig. 'I'd knock into his feet but he'd knock it straight back. It kept happening,' added Roy, who ended up getting plenty of the ball at Wembley.

Bobby watched from the sidelines. He didn't come on as a substitute, preferring to offer his services as sponge man in case anyone got a knock. His re-experiencing of the scene of his greatest triumph remained a mostly vicarious one. Bobby had played at Wembley for a second time in the resulting Charity Shield in 1976. He could have been forgiven for champing at the bit to get another taste of playing there, even if he had long retired, just to go to the end he scored at. But he didn't. He preferred to forego the opportunity in order for someone else to experience it.

It's unlikely Bobby has ever been compared to German fashion designer Karl Lagerfeld, who confesses to loving chocolate despite not having eaten it for more than 30 years. For a man who pays close attention to what he eats, Lagerfeld satisfies his craving from nothing more than the smell of chocolate. He will bring a bar towards his mouth, but only to draw in its scent. Bobby was the same. He was at Wembley to breathe it in, rather than gorge himself silly on the memory. 'He was the kind of guy you'd do anything for. I think he'd do the same for me,' said Roy.

24

Full English

THOSE looking to escape the cold wind coming in off Portsmouth harbour in the 1990s could find shelter in the nearby Harbour View Café where Bobby worked. His cousin Maria owned the café. She got Bobby to join her – he cooked and served customers. 'He worked seven days a week,' said Maria. 'He didn't have to work those hours but he wanted to.' The exact details of Bobby's whereabouts were still lost on some who knew him. Bobby Stokes? Oh yeah, he worked in that sandwich bar. No, he flipped burgers in a place in Gosport. The Harbour View Café is neither of those things – it's an old-fashioned greasy spoon on the Hard Interchange, a transport hub next to Portsmouth Harbour train station and the ferry terminal to Gosport. People go there to go somewhere else – either to leave the city or explore it further. Or at least you could. It was demolished in 2015 – its presence deemed no longer in keeping with the newly-developed Portsmouth waterfront.

You could get a decent cup of coffee and a sausage sandwich there for a couple of quid. A cardboard sign

Blu-Tacked to the wall encouraged customers to part with 50p for well-thumbed paperbacks by Chris Ryan and Rosamunde Pilcher stacked beneath on a trolley. Customers were more inclined to flick through the tabloids, while a transistor radio played golden oldies, like 'I Can See for Miles' by The Who, and 'Silence is Golden' by The Tremeloes. Some of the customers were on first-name terms with the ladies behind the counter. Customers tended to leave as they arrived – in pockets. When they left the café was empty. The fizzy drinks chest seemed to hum that bit louder. Outside, people walked purposefully to flag a taxi or catch a train. Inside it could be quiet; providing plenty of time to be alone with your thoughts.

John Robson's work with Bobby had runs its course but the two remained in touch. Sometimes John would pop into the café to see Bobby. He caught Bobby's eye as the bell sounded on the door on his entrance. Bobby signalled he'd take a break to have a quick cuppa with his old mate at one of the cafe's thin Formica tables. They made small talk as Bobby looked down at his mug of steaming hot tea. 'One day we were talking and he was telling me that the café made a fortune – they charged the best part of a quid for a cup of tea, but it only cost them a few pence to make,' said John.

From that moment the seed of an idea was planted. Why didn't the pair open up their own café? Bobby was very good with the customers and he could cook. He also already had a job with Maria at the Harbour View. 'Although they never said anything about it I knew,' said Maria. 'John used to come to the café quite often and I would say, "What are you two up to?" John would be a bit embarrassed sometimes – he'd ask for a coffee and I'd say, "That'll be 60p please. You'll be charging me when you open yours won't you."' Maria didn't mention the subject in front of Bobby, she didn't feel she needed to.

This wasn't pub talk, it was serious. John and Bobby spoke about it at length in the coming weeks, exchanging ideas. The idea grew into a business plan. They found a plot next to a hairdresser's at the top of Shirley high street, which was within walking distance from The Dell. John would leave Waterlooville and pick Bobby up. 'We'd spoken regularly about it,' said John. 'He was keen as mustard.' They both agreed to name the café The 83rd Minute – a nod to when Bobby's Wembley goal was scored. They planned how it would look, with photographs of Bobby's career hung on the wall. 'We were going to do it right,' said John. 'Start off with sandwiches and hot drinks, get our names out there.' It would obviously become a hub for Saints fans, who could say they had a chat with Bobby in the week leading up to, or maybe on matchday. John had the finances all worked out – it would cost something in the region of £15,000, an outlay he estimated they could recoup in around six months.

Bobby's wife was pleased, relieved even. Finally this could be the project that would focus Bobby's energy, he could be around football people and use his past as leverage for earning some money for his future. John was honest. He saw the project as a great opportunity for himself, as well as helping out a friend. It never happened. 'Bobby got cold feet a week before we were due to go in and do the work,' said John. 'He had doubts and asked me if I thought the whole thing was really a good idea.' John and his wife thought it was a great idea. So did Bobby's wife. 'He couldn't go ahead with it,' added John. 'He didn't want people thinking look at me I'm Bobby Stokes.' John was devastated as he felt the place would have been a hit. The spurned venture didn't spoil their friendship. Sometimes John would go looking for a reaction, telling Bobby that the two of them stood to earn a fortune. Bobby never bit back.

Bobby remained at the Harbour View Café. It was a short bus ride to the café from his house in Southsea. The buses ran on a different timetable on Sunday so he got a lift in from Ken Taylor. Now in his 80s, Ken has a neatly-trimmed moustache like Clark Gable in *Gone with the Wind*. He has been a season ticket holder at Portsmouth for years. He's seen it all at the club: from back-to-back titles to relegation to the Fourth Division, then back up to the Premier League and seeing the club win the FA Cup and then back down to the bottom tier again.

Ken was superintendent at The Hard. He was in charge of overseeing what was a hub for tourism. For some, arriving at The Hard, perhaps unsure on directions, it was their first experience of Portsmouth. Ken wanted people going away feeling like they'd been looked after. The Hard was brand new in 1979. An aerial photograph of it hangs on the wall of the spare room in his house, which is around the corner from Fratton Park. Ford Sierras in the foreground of the picture betray a different era. The café is just part of the main building. He points to the roof terrace, explaining that an Italian family used to have an ice-cream parlour there. 'It's not the same down there now,' said Ken, shortly before they pulled the place down. 'It's suffered from a lack of investment.'

Ken liked to get to work a bit early to keep himself organised with a cup of tea. On Sunday mornings he would wait in his car for Bobby on Aston Road. 'Sometimes I'd have to wait for a while,' said Ken. 'Bobby would lock his front door behind him, then unlock it and go back inside. He'd do that six times sometimes.' Ken asked Bobby what was wrong. 'He told me he was worried about fires, so he liked to make sure everything was unplugged.' The words of Bobby's dad telling John Robson he would do anything to avoid responsibility rang true. Faced with the responsibility of locking up the house, Bobby seemed preoccupied with the possibility of returning to a home that was burnt to the ground.

Ken knew Bobby's wife was a professional dancer – she travelled around the world as a dance examiner. So one day in the car Ken asked Bobby why he didn't go with her. 'Bobby replied that he'd had his good days,' said Ken. 'And that now it was her time to have a turn.' That remark stuck with Ken and he thought it was a touching thing to say. Ken was very much aware of Bobby's footballing career but it didn't crop up in conversation. 'Bobby was no show-off, but he came to life with any attention about his glory days,' added Ken, who always felt Bobby was thrown crumbs by the football establishment. 'Bobby held Mick Channon in very high regard – idolised him. He thought Southampton were planning a testimonial for him and that would have meant the world to him. I think it was disgraceful Bobby never received a testimonial, especially as he had earned the Golden Boot.' A testimonial was eventually planned for Bobby, but it would be too late for him.

25

Quiet Goodbye

SOMEBODY had taken it upon themselves to stove Brian O'Neil's skull in with a crowbar. Just why has never been made clear. Brian was fighting for his life in hospital in the north-east. The news quickly filtered south, with Bobby going up to visit. John Robson was a native of County Durham and he drove Bobby north along with John's brother-in-law. They packed accordingly for the long drive with sufficient rounds of sandwiches in Tupperware lunch boxes. Bobby had his own dietary requirements, preferring instead to take a six-pack of beer.

The journey required several comfort breaks; passengers needed fresh air and the space to stretch their restless legs. John made a penultimate stop at Oakenshaw, a small mining village in the heartlands of his home county. The mining industry had all but died, reducing the village to something of an outpost. Until recently constituents wishing to vote in elections did so at a polling station which was effectively a caravan, which has since been replaced by a mustard yellow Portakabin. The passengers soon returned to John's car. But Bobby was missing. It was long before the days of mobile phones, so they had little alternative but to comb the area on foot. They split up and covered everywhere, including all the pubs. Nothing. John racked his brains. They couldn't drive off without him, where was he?

There was one place left, the Welfare Miners' club. John knew the bar staff there. As soon as he walked in he heard that familiar 'Ampsher twang interspersed with a series of soft Durham accents. Bobby had been spotted walking through the village by Peter Hemingway, a local who was a big football fan. He stopped Bobby in the street to ask him two questions: was he Bobby Stokes? And if so did he fancy a pint? It was music to Bobby's ears. By the time John arrived at the bar, Bobby was sat down with a drink, surrounded by a circle of 20 or so chairs which seated the small impromptu audience of local football fans who wanted to take this unlikely opportunity to talk to Bobby about the game and in particular, the 1976 FA Cup Final. Bobby's goal continued to resonate, not just with those in the red and white half of Hampshire but far beyond. As this incident demonstrated, Bobby was as recognisable the best part of six hours north up the M1 as he was in Southampton. In this setting, of no fixed schedule or conversational itinerary, he seemed quite content.

Brian made a miraculous recovery. He had improved significantly by the time Bobby came to see him, but he was further galvanised by his visit. What would galvanise Bobby? He was moving in ever-decreasing circles. By 1994 word had got round all was not as well as it could have been with him. Southampton awarded him a benefit year that was due to climax in a testimonial match at The Dell in 1995. Bobby would be given the money generated from ticket sales. He confessed to being disappointed to not have been given a testimonial while he was still a Southampton player in the late 1970s. It caused him to eventually pick up the telephone to the club and ask for one. By the 90s Denis Bundy was the matchday compere in the Executive Club at The Dell. Part of his role was to interview players after the game. As a fan of the club, he loved it. He remembers that it was Peter Osgood's idea to do a testimonial for Bobby – the two had remained close friends. Although Bobby was reported to have made the call to ask for a testimonial, it's difficult to imagine him doing so. If he couldn't ask a colleague for work how could he ask his former employees for this – the last pay day? It's more likely Peter Osgood had poked the fire first. Lawrie McMenemy was back at the club as director of football, he then relayed the idea to the board and it was accepted.

Peter had already persuaded Denis to get Bobby involved at The Dell. Denis used to pick him up on matchdays. 'Bobby sat with me in the special executive area of the West Stand. They'd announce it over the PA that he was there and people would turn around and clap – he loved it, but Bobby was different from a lot of ex-professionals,' said Denis. 'He was very modest and shy and I don't think he ever quite understood why he was so popular at the club and with so many fans.'

The Dell was surrounded by housing. Denis used to park at a nearby primary school on matchdays as youngsters would be poised around the main stadium car park, waiting for players to arrive so they could pounce upon them to get an autograph. They wouldn't have been old enough to remember Bobby, but their dads were. It was they who sent their children after Bobby as he arrived at the gates. They would sacrifice the opportunity to make small talk with the club's playing contingent including Jon Gittens and Micky Adams, sprinting past them in hot pursuit of Bobby, who had no problem using Denis's bonnet as a makeshift desk to sign their books and programmes, even if he was a little unsure why they would want it. 'He would never say no to an autograph,' added Denis. 'No matter how many were in the queue.'

Denis shared further observations on Bobby's seeming inability, or perhaps lack of interest, in the material trappings of his FA Cup Final winner. He was once having a cup of tea at Bobby's house. As a Southampton fan, curiosity and opportunity got the better of him – where was his golden boot, the one he was presented with for scoring that goal? Denis had already scanned the living room, it was not on any plinth on the mantelpiece. Bobby took a moment to think, he didn't know exactly where it was.

He asked his wife – she didn't know either. He started ferreting about in the cupboard under the stairs. It was stashed away behind the vacuum cleaner. 'Only a few of those boots exist and Bobby wasn't sure where his was,' said Denis. 'He had it in his hand and he was saying, "It's all right, innit." It was the same with his cup winner's medal. Again, he had to go and find it. It was hidden away in a drawer.' To Denis it was amazing to hold both those items. 'It didn't quite equate to Bobby,' he added.

Denis headed up the committee with Peter Osgood to run Bobby's benefit year, which was a planned series of dinners and functions in the lead-up to the match at the end of the 1994/95 season. He had plenty of experience running cricketers' benefit years so he took Bobby to a few dinners to show him how it worked. It was an introduction to the world of the after-dinner speaking circuit that many ex-players turned to in order to earn part of their living. For those who were able it was a pretty straightforward gig. A famous former footballer talking to a roomful of fans who used to pay to watch them play was not a tough crowd – they were preaching to the choir. Public speaking was a walk in the park for Peter, who could talk the hind legs off a donkey. Stand him up in front of an audience and he'd happily hold court all evening about yesteryear. Bobby just wasn't like that.

Denis had already given Bobby a taste of this at the Executive Club. He'd bring him up on stage and introduce him. It was no good shoving a microphone in Bobby's face – it wasn't natural to him to take the lead, but if he was coaxed into it as a talking guest then he was fine. Denis decided to make it into a question-and-answer format, bringing him up to the stage before the match and asking him where he thought the danger was coming from the opposition, that kind of thing. The idea of being centre stage at his benefit dinners made Bobby a little anxious and nervous. He'd have to have a drink to settle his nerves.

Lawrie McMenemy remembers Bobby being somewhat embarrassed by it all. 'He wasn't comfortable that people were there to help him financially. We let him know it was not a hand-out, it was out of respect and for what he achieved for the football club,' said Lawrie, who noticed a notable change in Bobby's appearance: 'He looked thin, his shirt was loose around his neck.' His flagging health didn't stop Bobby from looking the part. 'He was never scruffy,' said Denis. 'He was always smartly turned out, but he never changed – his hair remained long all his life and he didn't seem at all bothered by working in a café, but he needed the security a successful testimonial would have provided. Peter Osgood wanted the dinners to be a success more than anybody and he became protective of Bobby. Bobby liked a drink and sometimes it would cause others to have a quiet word. I remember Ossie giving him a proper telling-off because he was drinking too much at one of the dinners. It was like being told off by your dad,' said Denis. 'Ossie was extremely fond of Bobby, but he would always tell him if he thought he was in the wrong.'

These functions didn't provide the same relaxed environment as a casual drink at the pub. They carried customs and protocol. The dress code was smart, and business cards would be exchanged as frequently as any banter. Such networking was how people got on. Bobby was there to sell nostalgia – albeit for his own benefit – but he was no salesman. Rumours circulated of him being too unwell to finish a round of golf. Then his wife left. The pain of the split hit both of them but it was Bobby's wound to suture. It was he who had to adapt to a new way of life. Perhaps if he was able to do so his wife would return and end what he hoped would only be a temporary separation. His good nature made him universally popular and well thought of – it was also the characteristic that seemed to snare him. It did not allow him the necessary quota of self-importance to take some of the post-football-career opportunities that came his way. Not because of any self-indulgent or self-destructive streaks within him, but a kink within his reasoning that didn't allow him to believe he was worthy of it all.

The circumstances he was facing weren't unique. It was because of this that not too many were too concerned about Bobby's plight. They believed he could navigate the choppy waters of a broken relationship while struggling through the tricky years of post-football retirement, which was a familiar story for ex-professional footballers from the 1970s. Although it was known that Bobby wasn't looking after himself as he should have done, those close to him believed his benefit year would provide him with a clean slate, an opportunity for him to move on and build a new life.

Bobby gave few clues to the reality. He wasn't prone to pouring his heart out over his personal life. Not once did he use the trips with Denis up and down the M27 to divulge the breakdown of his marriage. 'In all the time I knew Bobby I never heard him say a bad word against anyone – he was just a lovely bloke,' said Denis. 'He loved a drink and was always a heavy smoker and I really think it all took its toll. The FA Cup was obviously very special and the testimonial would have been brilliant, but they were no replacement for the ultimate sadness in his private life.'

It was through living alone that Bobby was unable to moderate his lifestyle or able to see a future. There was no one to say no, then it was too late. Sometimes Maria Johnson would go for a drink with Bobby after work. 'Bob liked a pint,' said Maria. 'But people used to knock him for it and I got a bit uptight about that because they were often the ones who wanted to meet him in the pub. So I'd ask them why they were meeting him in the pub if they had so much to say about it.' They went because Bobby would often buy their drinks.

In the early months of 1995, Roy Beazley got a telephone call from Bobby. He told Roy that he wasn't feeling well and thought it was his heart. Roy worked at Southampton General Hospital, so he organised an appointment for Bobby, who caught the train from Portsmouth to Southampton Central. Roy collected him. It's just under three miles from Southampton Central train station to the hospital but you have to go through several sets of traffic lights on Shirley high street to get there. Bobby had a full scan. 'They checked everything,' said Roy. When it was finished the consultant wanted a word with Bobby; he was frank, telling him he needed to completely alter his lifestyle. Roy gave Bobby a lift back to the station. He wanted to know what Bobby was going to do. Bobby shrugged, telling Roy he'd cut down on drinking and the cigarettes. Roy pleaded with him, 'Cut down? You've got to stop.' He then watched Bobby close the passenger door and make his way towards the platform. It was the last time he would see him. Within a few months he was dead.

Bobby's yellow and blue Southampton jersey from the 1976 FA Cup Final was folded up in a carrier bag in

Denis Bundy's office. It still had the grass stains on it from Wembley. Denis had never planned to keep it. The idea was to get Bobby to sign it and then auction it off at his final benefit dinner at Southampton Guildhall. Bobby had suggested he auction off his winner's medal, but Denis and Peter Osgood convinced him to keep it. Bobby hadn't invested any sentiment in it.

Denis remembers Bobby being really chuffed with the £2,000 they'd raised for him at the previous benefit dinners. He remains adamant that Bobby's framed shirt and golden boot would have gone for fortunes and that all in all they'd have made him in the region of £15,000 to £20,000, which would have been significant in 1995. After Bobby's death, Denis returned the shirt and golden boot to Bobby's wife Janet. The testimonial match never took place as everything went flat without him. He would always talk about his famous moment, but only if asked. He was caught in a vicious circle as the thing trying to help him – the benefit year – was the thing he found difficult to deal with, in that talking about himself as if he was a hero, if only for the benefit of his testimonial, was impossible for him.

Mick Channon once said that in one way Bobby was too nice to be a footballer. Nice is a word that is regularly used to describe Bobby. He met what was seen as a tragic end, but to those who knew him he was anything but a tragic figure. Although his time was far shorter than anyone would choose to have, the impact his life had while he was here is still keenly felt, not just because of that famous goal but the way he was as a person – a modest lad from Paulsgrove who slipped Portsmouth's net and created celebrations in Southampton that have yet to be seen since the days that followed a Saturday afternoon in May in 1976.

Years later, after Bobby's parents had passed away, the new residents at 63 Leominster Road found a bag in the attic. It was filled with newspaper cuttings from Bobby's footballing career, no doubt collected over the years by his parents and secured in the safety of the loft before time took them both. How it came to escape the dustbin demonstrates how 'Grovers stick together, with a sense of communal spirit that does still exist.

Helen Harris's neighbour walked her dog with the new residents at number 63 and word got back to Helen about the bag of bric-a-brac that she cannot bring herself to look at for risk of opening up old wounds. So while clues to Bobby remain in small ways in Southampton and Portsmouth, he is, were it not for some community spirit, almost impossible to find. Not so much lost as hidden. Maybe that's how Bobby preferred it. Or at least that is how he was probably more comfortable. Now he is no longer with us we don't have to follow those wishes so explicitly. After all, he scored the winning goal in an FA Cup Final. Have you?

Bibliography

All the Saints: A Complete Who's Who of Southampton FC, by Gary Chalk, Duncan Holley, and David Bull. *Published by Hagiology Publishing, 2013.*

Constant Paine: From Southampton Legend to South African Ambassador, by David Bull. *Published by Hagiology Publishing, 2008.*

Saints v Pompey: A History of Unrelenting Rivalry, by Dave Juson, Clay Aldworth, David Bull, Gary Chalk and Barry Bendel. *Published by Hagiology Publishing, 2004.*

Seventeen miles from Paradise: Saints v Pompey - Passion, Pride and Prejudice, by Colin Farmery. *Published by Desert Island Football Histories, 2004.*

Southampton's Cult Heroes: Saints' 20 Greatest Icons, by Jeremy Wilson. *Published by Know the Score Books, 2006*

Tie a yellow ribbon: How Saints won the cup, by Tim Manns and David Bull. *Published by Hagiology Publishing, 2008.*

Plus author interviews with:

Roy Beazley
Lenny Benham
Paul Bennett
Mel Blyth
Greg Brown
Martin Buchan
Denis Bundy
Mick Channon

Mike Channon junior
Ray Crawford
Peter Denyer
Mike Dillon
Don Divers
Gary Edwards
Hughie Fisher
Roger Fry

BOBBY STOKES

Jimmy Gabriel
Paul Gilchrist
Ray Graydon
Albie Harris
Helen Harris
Steve Hatton
Maurice Hewlett
Denis Hollywood
Nick Holmes
Steve Horner
Bill Irwin
Maria Johnson
Dave Kemp
Carmine Marcantino
Neil Marchant
Eric Martin
Jim McCalliog
Don McAllister
Bob McCarthy
Lawrie McMenemy
Mark Newman

Tommy O'Hara
Brian O'Neil
Terry Paine
Norman Piper
Maitland Pollock
Jim Reed
David Reynolds
Neil Rioch
John Robson
Chris Sibley
Kevin Sibley
Gordon Smith
Jim Steele
Alex Stepney
Ian St John
Ken Taylor
Ruth Taylor
Keith Viney
Kevin Wallace
Trevor Wallis